Why Most Investors Fail and Why You Don't Have To

Simple, Tax-Efficient Strategies That Control Risk, Eliminate Confusion, and Turn the Odds of Success in Your Favor

Michael Jon Allen

iUniverse LLC
Bloomington

WHY MOST INVESTORS FAIL AND WHY YOU DON'T HAVE TO
SIMPLE, TAX-EFFICIENT STRATEGIES THAT
CONTROL RISK, ELIMINATE CONFUSION, AND
TURN THE ODDS OF SUCCESS IN YOUR FAVOR

iUniverse books may be ordered through booksellers or by contacting:

iUniverse LLC
1663 Liberty Drive
Bloomington, IN 47403
www.iuniverse.com
1-800-Authors (1-800-288-4677)

Because of the dynamic nature of the Internet, any web addresses or links contained in this book may have changed since publication and may no longer be valid. The views expressed in this work are solely those of the author and do not necessarily reflect the views of the publisher, and the publisher hereby disclaims any responsibility for them.

Any people depicted in stock imagery provided by Thinkstock are models, and such images are being used for illustrative purposes only.
Certain stock imagery © Thinkstock.

ISBN: 978-1-4917-1742-4 (sc)
ISBN: 978-1-4917-1744-8 (hc)
ISBN: 978-1-4917-1743-1 (e)

Library of Congress Control Number: 2013922297

Printed in the United States of America.

iUniverse rev. date: 01/16/2014

CONTENTS

CHAPTER 1

Why Most Investors Fail and Why You Don't Have To

The vast majority of investors—professionals and amateurs alike—fail at investing.

The thesis of this book is that most people fail because no matter their educational backgrounds or levels of investing experience, human beings are too easily impressed by elegant theories that have little to no basis in fact. We are hardwired to see patterns that do not really exist. And we are intellectually lazy. If something is repeated often enough, we very easily take for granted that it is true without truly questioning the underlying premises.

In this book, I hope to show you first and foremost how to avoid being misled by elegant theories. What matters most is that you never take conventional wisdom for granted. Hopefully, you will quickly learn to recognize the flaws in any investment thesis, and you will be able to ask the right questions needed to get at the real truth.

Let's start with a completely make-believe story to illustrate one of the most important points of this book. Suppose I am starting a new airline company based on my belief that the time you spend traveling to your vacation should be as enjoyable as the time you spend at your destination. I'm so convinced that if you ride my airline just once, you will never fly with any other airline, so I'm giving away a hundred pairs of free tickets to any destination in the world. There are no set travel dates as long as you fly within the next twelve months, and I will even throw in one week's room and board at the luxury hotel of your choice. Would you like to take advantage of this offer?

Most readers will probably say yes even if they have no intention of paying the premium prices I charge for travel on my luxury airliners. Some will wonder if there isn't some kind of hidden cost, but it is just too easy to be cynical. I guarantee there are no hidden costs and no hidden agendas, so just get that out of your head. My objective is straightforward and simple: I want to get you to try my service so you will become as convinced as I am that it is the only way to fly.

It's entirely free, and you can go wherever you want to go whenever you want to go there. Now are you interested? Good.

But what if I then told you that our planes frequently encounter mechanical difficulties and that as a result there is at least a 25 percent chance you will not reach your destination? Would you still take the tickets? Probably not.

Yet this is exactly what you are doing when you buy the line from the typical stockbroker or financial advisor who tells you stocks have returned 11 percent annually and that you should never try to time the market. You've probably heard this story so many times before that you feel you have little reason to doubt their advice. But if you believe it, think about why you believe it. Have you actually gone back and measured for yourself? How did you get the information, and how did you verify it? Did you ask the broker or advisor where he or she got the information? Did you even stop to ask yourself why 11 percent instead of 9 percent or 15 percent? Is there anything magic about the number 11?

Some very simple research reveals that the number 11 is in fact a preposterous lie. It is one of the most common assumptions upon which almost all financial plans are based. It is hardwired into many of the leading software packages. The common yet false assumption is if that was the rate for fifty years, it must be a pretty reliable guide for long-term investors. This argument may seem intuitive, but it is totally illogical. There is simply no intrinsic reason whatsoever for the next fifty years to have any relationship to the previous fifty years.

The number 11 is not even correct when applied to the past. During the single most explosive fifty-year period in stock market history, stocks—as measured by the Standard & Poor's 500 Index (S&P 500)—returned on average just 10.5 percent annually. After inflation, this return was reduced to 7.1 percent annually. This was the best fifty-year period ever recorded; it included many overseas wars, but it did not include the three most devastating wars in our history. It included several recessions, but it did not include the three greatest depressions in our history. It also encompassed the period of the United States' transition from being a third-rate supplier of raw materials to the greatest superpower, both militarily and economically, the world has ever seen. There is simply no reason to presume this was a normal fifty years in the course of human history.

In fact, if you had instead bought stocks during the worst fifty-year period in our stock market's history, the total return would have been a mere 0.5 percent per year after inflation. How much difference does that make in a fifty-year period? If you had invested $100,000, you would have $3,104,934 of inflation-adjusted dollars at the end of the best fifty-year period, but at the end of the worst period, you would only have $126,370. In fact, after taxes, you would most likely have less than what you started with in real purchasing power.

There is no reason to use either of these periods as guides to the future. Neither of these scenarios represent the most likely outcome of your investments. In fact, there is no reason to use the past as a guide to the future at all. Any first-year statistical textbook will warn students that historical relationships do not imply causal relationships. In this case, the relationship being studied is between time and price. Whenever anyone suggests that stocks should go up at any particular rate for no other reason than that this was the rate achieved during some period in the past, then they are implying that the passage of time causes stocks to go up, which is of course absurd.

It appears to be true that the longer you hold stocks, the less likely you are to lose money, but risk does not fall off as quickly as most people assume. If you invest in a diversified portfolio of stocks at the end of any given month in any year, the likelihood of losing money during the next twelve months has been 38 percent historically. In the short term, stocks are hardly better than the toss of a coin. If you held those stocks for any given five-year period, the odds of losing real purchasing were still 33 percent. Ten years on, the odds of losing real money remained 27 percent, and after fifteen years, the odds were 23 percent. After twenty years, the odds of losing real purchasing power were still 19 percent.

A thorough and robust statistical analysis shows us that a far more likely mean total return per year for stocks over any randomly selected ten-year period is somewhere between 3 percent and 4 percent but that anything between –10 percent and +20 percent is perfectly plausible. It is this wide range of plausible outcomes that makes any one specific forecast unlikely and unrealistic.

If I told you that in the best possible scenario you could make 7.1 percent annually after inflation but that there was a 19 percent chance you would lose money, how much more careful would you want to be about investing than if I told you 9 percent was pretty much guaranteed? Probably a lot more careful. This is new information that should affect the way you behave as an investor. It doesn't necessarily mean you should never buy stocks, but it renders into absurdity any idea that you should always own stocks.

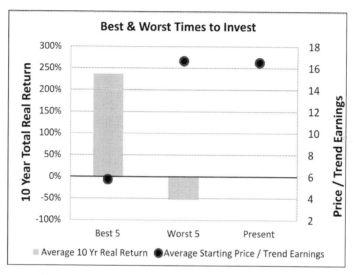

Chart 1: Long-term returns on stocks vary dramatically depending on when you invest and how much you pay.

Why Most Market Timers Fail

While it is true that if you don't time the market, you are doomed to fail, unfortunately, even if you do time the market, your odds of success are extraordinarily low. A recent study by Dalbar of the last twenty years shows that investors in US stock mutual funds on average underperformed the benchmark S&P 500 by almost 4 percent per year (Harvey 2013). To put this into perspective, if you invested $10,000 in an index fund and $10,000 in the average investor's portfolio, at the end of this period, the index fund would be worth $25,467 more than the average investor's portfolio. The Dalbar study actually underestimates the difference, because index fund investors pay very little in taxes, while the average investor pays very dearly.

A study by researchers at the University of California (UoC) at Davis during a much shorter period of five years found that while the average investor underperformed the benchmark by about 2 percent annually after commissions and fees, those who traded more than 9 percent of their portfolio annually actually gave up 10 percent a year in performance (Barber 2003). Using our same example of the $10,000 portfolios, that kind of underperformance leads to a $5,800 difference in just five years. The UoC Davis study also failed to account for taxes and was conducted during a period when the types of stocks favored by individual investors actually outperformed the benchmark.

Unfortunately, most professional market timers are not any better than individuals. The Hulbert Financial Digest tracks 305 market-timing strategy newsletters, and whether one looks at short-term or long-term performance, only about 22 percent outperform their benchmarks on a risk-adjusted basis, and even then the achievement is extremely dubious. Most of the gains are in reduced volatility. Very few—indeed, fewer than a handful—actually achieve better absolute performance, and no matter what your tax bracket, I found only one out of the entire database that achieved better after-tax returns.

Why Most Mutual Funds Fail

So how do professional long-term investors do? Lipper Analytics monitors the performance of 23,866 mutual funds that have track records for ten years or longer. During the past ten years, fewer than 16 percent of these funds outperformed the S&P 500, which is the core benchmark index by which most of these funds either are or should be measured. The odds that you will be able to choose even one of these winning funds are extremely low. The probability that you will fill your entire portfolio with winning funds is effectively zero.

But let's say you are one of the really smart people who concentrate their money in one of those market-beating funds. Don't worry. You will still be doomed. Unfortunately, if you own a mutual fund, or if you invest on your own by following almost any newsletter or trading system ever designed, there is almost a 100 percent probability that you are paying so much in taxes that any performance advantage is destroyed.

Stocks have the most favorable tax status of all liquid investments because capital gains can be deferred until actual profits are realized, which means you can make 15 percent or 35 percent or even 100 percent profit in any given year, but unless you actually sell the stock, these gains are completely tax-free. If you own a stock and never sell it, you never have to pay any taxes on the profits. Warren Buffett calls this an interest-free loan from the government because all the while you owe these taxes, you are accruing additional capital gains free of any charges. While you own this stock, you collect ever-increasing dividends and only pay 15 percent tax on the dividends, which in most cases will be lower than the tax you pay on any other form of income. If you ever do sell the stock, you only pay 15 percent on the gains.

Most mutual funds destroy this advantage. According to Morningstar data, the average mutual fund in America turns over 95 percent of its portfolio every year. You will effectively pay taxes on all your gains in every year, and unavoidably, a large share of these gains will be counted as short-term capital gains, which are taxed at the normal income tax rate. If you are in a very high tax bracket, this can be disastrous, but even if you are at a marginal rate of 25 percent, you would need to outperform the market by 2.3 percent annually to make up the difference caused by this premature taxation. Since the S&P 500 returned 8.16 percent during the past ten years, a mutual fund would have needed to achieve 29.6 percent before taxes during the same time to make the equivalent after-tax return.

When I started writing this book, there was not a single fund in the Lipper database that even came close to clearing this hurdle rate. The closest match was the Black Rock Latin America Fund with 21.62 percent. Interestingly, about 99 percent of the funds that achieved more than 15 percent total returns were in the emerging markets category, and most of these were specialized in Latin American–related equities, while a few specialized in Asian emerging markets. Emerging markets account for less than 5 percent of global market capitalization, so these are extremely specialized funds, and anyone concentrating their portfolios in these funds at the beginning of the decade would have been considered extremely imprudent.

The chance you will ever be able to pick a general equity fund that can outperform the market after taxes for more than a decade is actually lower than your odds of winning the lottery.

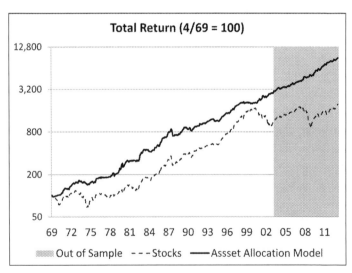

Chart 2: A simple asset allocation model using only five Index ETFs has returned more than treble the stock market total returns over the past four decades with significantly less volatility.

Why Most Stock Pickers Fail

The second biggest lie on Wall Street is that ordinary people can pick stocks successfully in their spare time. I blame Peter Lynch for starting this nonsense with his 1989 best seller, *One Up on Wall Street* (Lynch 1989), in which he argued that amateur investors could reap exceptional rewards from mundane, easy-to-understand companies they encountered in their daily lives. Since then, American investors have become the most active individual investors in the world, and a trillion-dollar industry has sprung up to support them. But an interesting study recently published by BlackRock proves the folly of this theory. From 1993 to 2011, eighteen years that almost coincide with the time since Lynch's book was first published, the average individual underperformed the index by an extraordinary 4.1 percent per year (Blackrock 2012). In that amount of time, an index fund buy-and-hold investor could have turned $100,000 into $320,714, but the average investor turned it into only $148,595.

But let's say you are a true genius, and unlike almost anyone else, you have an ability to consistently beat the market. You might still be using your time very foolishly.

Remember, you can buy an index fund and do nothing, and you will make the market rate. You can also probably make extra money by tending bar or delivering newspapers or writing a blog about your most favorite thing in the world. So to compensate you for any time you spend trying to beat the market, you need to measure the amount of money you make in excess of the market rate divided by the number of hours you spend doing it. You should then compare this to the rate you could make doing other jobs. You don't necessarily need to make as much as you would from the other jobs. If stock picking is what you enjoy most and you don't mind making less money, I'm not one to judge you. But even if you invest for a hobby, you need to do the math so you know how much your hobby is really costing you.

Just because you made 20 percent one year does not justify your time spent if the market went up 27 percent that year. You could have put the money in an index fund and been on the beach, sipping piña coladas the whole time, and you would have made more money. This kind of a year would be more like an internship in which you paid 7 percent of your assets for the privilege of doing work, except that an internship usually enhances your resume.

Let's say you make 6 percent more than the market every year and have $50,000 to invest. If the market goes up 10 percent, you would make $5,000 in an index fund, but since you're so smart, you make $8,000. Let's assume that this extra $3,000 per year is what you can make consistently every year. But how much time do you have to spend executing that system, and how much do you think your time is worth? The average worker in the United States made about $23 an hour in 2011; so for $3,000, you should be willing to work about 130 hours, or roughly thirty minutes per weekday.

But what if your system is not consistent? What if some years you actually underperform the market? No one is perfect. Would you still be willing to put in the same thirty minutes a day for this kind of work? To compensate for the kind of risk you are taking, you would probably want to make at least two times and probably more like three times as much per hour as you could at a job that pays a regular wage. This means either you can only afford to spend ten minutes a day on your stock-picking job or you need to beat the market by 18 percent annually.

Here comes the gut check Peter Lynch did not tell you about: There are hundreds of thousands of professional investors with Ivy League postgraduate degrees and millions of dollars in equipment and research budgets who spend anywhere from ten to sixteen hours a day researching and trading stocks and other investable assets all over the world, and not a single one of them has ever beat the market by 6 percent annually in every year of his or her career. Ask yourself if it really makes any sense to believe you can compete with these people by spending ten minutes a day researching stocks on the Internet. I'm assuming you know that not everything you read on the Internet is true.

With all due respect to Peter Lynch, whose book is one of the most important books I have ever read as a professional investor, no one can do the things he advocates with only ten minutes a day of research. It's a complete fantasy. My most earnest suggestion is that unless you spend more than ten hours a day at it, you should forget about picking stocks for all but a very small portion of your portfolio. Maybe you have one or two really good ideas that you happen to be an expert in and it just wouldn't make sense not to take advantage of your specialty. That's fine. But even the most intelligent and knowledgeable experts are seriously wrong with alarming frequency. Keep your stock selections to a very bare minimum; you'll have to work out for your own situation what a bare minimum is, but it should be a level of investment in which being completely wrong will not hurt you. Trying to play the stock market in your spare time just isn't a smart way to make money.

There are some stock-picking strategies on the market that claim to take less time and still beat the markets consistently. The most well-known can be classified into two basic camps: value strategies and momentum strategies. Some combine both methodologies. Computer-driven strategies are highly appealing because they give the impression of being scientific and therefore immune to human emotions. Once again, we come up against the dangerous assumption that because something worked before, it should automatically work again. In most cases, there is simply no validity to these assumptions.

Once in a while, an apparent exception to the rule appears to show interesting potential. Many of these claim to have extremely long track records, and computer-simulated returns can easily make them seem more robust than they really are. For example, it is well-known that stocks with high book value to price consistently outperform the market. Somewhat less well-known is the fact that this outperformance is always driven by a relatively small number of stocks within the portfolio that perform spectacularly well—sometimes several hundred percent—lifting the rest of an otherwise very unspectacular group of stocks. To gain the same advantage, you must buy all the stocks in the recommended portfolio and follow all the trading rules precisely. In many cases, this implies owning hundreds of stocks and having your eyes on the portfolio every minute of every day the market is open.

Large institutions can afford to follow such strategies because they typically pay less than 0.06 percent in commissions for each trade and run hundreds of millions of dollars, so the cost of even very highly paid traders is trivial compared to the assets employed. If you are an individual investor paying $8 per trade, you would have to have a portfolio worth a minimum of $1.3 million to get the same trading efficiencies for a portfolio of one hundred stocks.

The Dogs of the Dow strategy is a well-known attempt to simplify the value strategy for use with very small portfolios. The Dogs of the Dow strategy chooses the highest yielding ten stocks from the Dow Industrials. Since you only need ten stocks, if you are willing to tolerate slightly higher costs, say 0.13 percent per trade, you can trade this strategy efficiently with only about $60,000. This strategy makes intuitive sense because it does a fairly good job of eliminating one of the most important defects of a value-based strategy.

Stocks always become cheapest before they go bankrupt. This happens to small stocks with greater frequency than it does to large stocks, so a broadly diversified value-based strategy will always include a disproportionately large share of companies that fail as businesses. If you could eliminate the stocks destined for the dustbin of history, there should be a better chance for the strategy to work. According to the Motley Fool, the only company to be removed from the Dow in its one-hundred-year history because of financial difficulties was the Johns Manville company. The Motley Fool article is undated, but clearly it was published before the removal of GM and Citicorp (Befumo & Schay). Still, three companies in more than one hundred years is a pretty reliable track record.

The Dogs of the Dow website (dogsofthedow.com) provides data indicating that this strategy has outperformed the S&P 500 by about 1.5 percent annually from 1996 to 2012, and it did so with significantly less volatility. This isn't a very long period of time to test a strategy because it only includes four down years, all in all just two bear markets. Still, the way the strategy fails rigorous testing even in this short period is instructive. During this period, the S&P 500 rose an average of 5.3 percent annually with a standard deviation of 18.8 percent. The Dogs of the Dow strategy reportedly returned 6.8 percent with a standard deviation of only 16.2 percent. But after transaction costs of only 0.13 percent per trade and capital gains taxes of only 15 percent, the total return of the Dogs of the Dow strategy was reduced to 4.9 percent.

The Little Book That Beats the Market by Joel Greenblatt follows a very similar strategy, but instead of dividends, it is based on low price-to-earnings (P/E) ratios, and instead of limiting the stocks to the Dow 30, it limits stocks to those with high returns on investment. *The Little Book* also recommends a more diversified portfolio—twenty to thirty stocks. Greenblatt claims that between 1988 and 2004, this strategy achieved 31 percent annually while the S&P returned only 12.4 percent (Greenblatt 2005). Other researchers, however, have been unable to replicate Greenblatt's results. Wes Gray's *Empirical Finance Blog* found only a 2.4 percent annual outperformance (Gray 2011), but this entire outperformance was attributable to just two years during the entire study. If you missed either of those years for any reason, you would have underperformed the market for the duration. Since there are more stocks in this strategy, there are also more expenses.

Investor's Daily founder Jim O'Neil takes a very different approach in his system, which reportedly made him a multimillionaire. His system attempts to identify companies with strong fundamentals—big sales and earnings increases that result from unique new products or services. These stocks are then bought when they emerge from price consolidation periods. Mistakes, which must be frequent, are sold automatically anytime cumulative losses exceed 7 percent of the original buying price.

Does the system really work? NorthCoast Advisors, which uses the same method with O'Neil's permission, publishes results on their website, which is regulated and therefore probably a little more reliable than *Investor's Daily*, which is free to print whatever it wants. The NorthCoast Asset Management website claims returns from 2005 through 2012 of 6.2 percent versus 4.6 percent for the S&P 500 with roughly half the volatility of the S&P 500. This performance is net of fees and transaction costs, but the high turnover of this strategy probably generates at least 1.5 percent drag from additional taxes on short-term gains. During this very short period, however, more than 100 percent of the outperformance was attributable to the system exiting the market in 2008. The actual stock-picking method underperformed the market considerably in nearly every year.

The story was more decisively negative when O'Neil tried to apply the system to his own mutual fund and failed on two separate occasions. His O'Neil Fund performed well in the 1966–1967 bull market but nosedived in 1968 and never recovered. He sold it in 1975 after it dropped to $6 million in assets from a peak of $49 million. When O'Neil again decided to close his New USA Growth Fund in 1997, it ranked 162 out of 276 growth funds tracked by Lipper Analytical Services over the five-year life of the fund.

The granddaddy of all public stock-picking methodologies is espoused by the Value Line Investment Survey, which since 1965 has made claims of superior performance that are difficult to refute. The survey covers 1,700 stocks, which it divides into five categories on a weekly basis. From 1965 to 2000, stocks ranked one and two nearly doubled the market's annualized return. Stocks ranked five were nearly half.

Unfortunately, the Value Line system requires a minimum portfolio size of one hundred names and a turnover rate of about 25 percent per month. Writing in the September 2000 issue of the *Journal of Financial and Quantitative Analysis*, James Choi concluded: "...there is no strong evidence that profitable abnormal returns can be realized from Value Line recommendations once transactions costs are taken into account" (Choi 2000).

Why Most Asset Allocators Fail

If most attempts to beat the market are futile, then many investors believe the best way to generate suitable long-term returns is to diversify across asset classes, of which stocks are only one of many available alternatives. Certainly, most investors know they should never put all their eggs in one basket, but the devil is in the details. Most investors overdiversify or diversify superficially. There are more than 28,000 mutual funds on the market, but the vast majority of them are for all intents and purposes identical. Holding a randomly selected sample of ten funds will serve no purpose whatsoever, but strategically selecting just a few can virtually eliminate 90 percent of the risk of investing.

You can achieve much more effective diversification with three funds that *all* behave differently in various circumstances than you can with twenty funds that are little different in anything but name. During the last real stress test of the markets, from November 2007 through March 2009, equities dropped 56 percent. At the same time, high-yield corporate bonds dropped 41 percent. High-quality corporate bonds dropped 24 percent. Preferred stocks dropped 56 percent. Real estate investment trusts dropped 66 percent. High-dividend stocks dropped 67 percent. Emerging market bonds dropped 33 percent.

These assets all had different names, and there was very little if any overlap in the actual holdings within each fund, but when a real emergency arose, they all behaved in the same manner. Despite the difference in names and investment objectives and despite the fact that they may have contained very different portfolios, they were all sensitive to the same economic factors.

Effective diversification requires finding the assets that react differently to the same economic factors. Successful asset allocation is extremely counterintuitive. To do it well, you must buy assets you expect will lose money, and you must sell assets you expect will make money. During the same November 2007 to March 2009 period highlighted above, cash, bonds, and gold all had positive returns. Holding just one stock fund along with these three other assets delivered far more diversification than a portfolio of ten or even fifteen different equity funds.

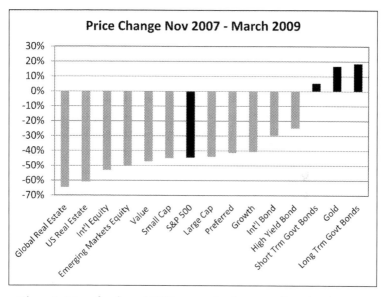

Chart 3: Most funds and ETFs move in the same direction because they share similar characteristics. Only asset classes that move in totally different directions are candidates for diversification strategies.

CHAPTER 2

The Five Keys to Changing the Odds

I hope you are sufficiently concerned by now. The conclusion you should be arriving at is that if you don't trade the markets, you are probably doomed. If you trade the markets on your own, you are also most likely doomed. If you seek professional advice to help with your trading, the odds are you're still doomed. If you let someone else trade for you, forget about it. You're just doomed.

There is a way to beat the odds, though, and it is surprisingly simple once you understand it. To be sure, it is not a method that is immediately obvious. If it were, everyone would be a millionaire. I've been investing professionally for more than twenty-five years, but it was only in the last thirteen years that I even began to focus on the most important data. Even then I was staring right at the answer for more than a decade before I figured out the key to unlocking consistent outperformance while reducing volatility at the same time. This discovery, and the process by which I capitalize on it, will be what the rest of this book is about.

The system you will learn about in this book will usually trade only about once or twice a year, and often it will only trade a small portion of your portfolio. Although you will generate some minor capital gains tax liabilities, they will almost always be long-term gains, which are typically taxed at only 15 percent at the time of this writing.

While the S&P generated 8.5 percent annually from 1970 to 2012, there were twelve down years, and the worst year was down more than 40 percent. If one had followed the model described in this book, however, the return would have averaged 11.3 percent with only four down years and no years in which the system lost more than 5.6 percent. You will not find it difficult to execute this system. In fact, you can probably make a large number of mistakes and still do well. Neither transaction costs nor fees are ever likely to eliminate the advantage.

Before starting, however, you should know that this system is based on a hypothetical model. Regulators frown on hypothetical models primarily because there is too much opportunity for fraud. Since hypothetical models have not actually been traded or audited by an independent entity, the modeler can pretty much say whatever he or she wants. But provided that the model is based on accurate data, fair assumptions, and sound methodologies, how ridiculous is it, really, to favor real performance of only a few years compared to a modeled performance of several decades?

There are five reasons why this model stands out from most other models:

1. *Simplicity*—Models that work well in theory are often impossible to execute in the real world either because of complexity, liquidity, or some other constraint. This model has no such constraints.

2. *History*—Most models are overspecified. In other words, they fit a specific time period too well and become inoperable whenever applied to any other time period. This model is intentionally underspecified.

3. *Foresight*—Many models are based purely on hindsight, which is always twenty-twenty. This model makes the effort to eliminate hindsight to a level that is extreme by any standard.
4. *Leverage*—Most models have only an on-and-off switch, so they can only add value when the market is going down. The only way for a model to outperform a rising market is to use leverage. This model does so very judiciously.
5. *Short-Selling*—Most models still lose money when the market is declining, or at least they do not make any money. Short-selling is considered too risky by most advisors, but mathematically the aversion to short-selling doesn't make sense. If the odds of the market going down are high, and they often are, then during such times short-selling is the least risky way to make money.

Simplicity

The most common reason regulators frown on the use of hypothetical returns is that hypothetical models often assume certain trades can be made whenever you want to make them at the price you want to make them. In the real world, stocks become illiquid and can't trade at any price. If a large fund tries to trade a small stock, it may be impossible to get the price that was used in the hypothetical returns. The cost of executing a strategy may be considerably higher than it was assumed on paper. I have seen hundreds of otherwise impressive-looking models destroyed by the insertion of a more reasonable expectation for costs.

I myself have failed to execute trades in the way proscribed by someone else's model. I was listening to one such trader on the phone as he made the trades. He claimed to have made money, and I lost money making the same exact trade at approximately the same minute of the day. It may have been that the model provider was a scam artist, or it may have been that I was a completely incompetent trader. Either way, a successful paper system that doesn't translate into real profits is useless.

Every time a trading system calls for the execution of a trade, there is an opportunity for execution error and increased cost. These issues are rendered immaterial in my system because the trades are so infrequent and the investment vehicles used are all tremendously liquid. There is virtually no possibility your trades will have any impact on the price. Trades are very minimal, so if you use a tax-efficient vehicle and a cost-efficient broker, your costs should be immaterial.

I take for granted that you will not always trade on the exact day the model calls for a change. I don't always get it right myself. The trades are infrequent enough and there are enough redundancies that these types of execution mistakes will not cause a serious deterioration in performance.

I use only a handful of exchange traded funds (ETFs) to execute the system. An ETF is a fund that holds assets such as stocks, bonds, or commodities but is traded on an exchange like a stock. They generally trade at a price close to the net asset value of underlying assets, so we do not ever have to concern ourselves with getting a fair price. Most ETFs track an index, such as the S&P 500, and individual assets within the ETF are hardly ever traded, so they are very cost-effective and tax-efficient.

The following are descriptions of the only five funds you will ever need to know about:

1. *SPY*—This fund seeks to match results of the S&P 500 Index. This will be our main tool for capitalizing on the tendency of US corporations to grow faster than the rate of inflation. We will buy and sell according to a model described in chapter 3.

2. *TLT*—This fund seeks to match the performance of the Barclays US 20+ Year Treasury Bond Index. This is the asset class we can rely on to perform best when the economy is weak and therefore to be uncorrelated and perhaps even inversely correlated to our holdings in SPY. We will buy and sell according to a model described in chapter 4.

3. *GLD*—This fund seeks to match the performance of the price of gold bullion. This asset class has a strong record of performing extremely well on the few occasions when both TLT and SPY are weak, which include but are not limited to periods of rapidly accelerating inflation. We will buy and sell according to the model described in chapter 5.

4. *BND*—This fund seeks to match the performance of a broad-based bond index, maintaining an average maturity consistent with that of the index, which ranges between five and ten years. This is a very low volatility index we will use as a default fund to switch assets into whenever the SPY or the GLD models are negative but the TLT model is positive.

5. *SHY*—This fund seeks to match the price and yield performance of the Barclays US One- to Three-Year Treasury Bond Index. You can use any money market fund in place of this fund and you will be fine. I use this fund in my models because it is easier to document.

Statistics

Human beings are programmed to jump to conclusions. We see patterns that do not really exist. In most cases, this ability to jump to conclusions has helped our species survive by enabling us to anticipate problems we would otherwise not be fast enough or strong enough to react to in time. We cringe at the sight of a bug, though most have no ability to harm us. We jump at the sight of a snake, though most are not poisonous. But when it comes to investments, this ability is often the cause of great harm. Because we made money in a particular kind of stock on a particular kind of signal, we suddenly think we know all there is to know about buying and selling any stock for all eternity. We think we know the pattern. In subsequent tries, whenever we fail, we blame the market for not following "the rules."

Even when a particular pattern is repeated two or three times, there is usually no rule or reason that requires the pattern to continue or be repeated. Most so-called stock market patterns are in reality nothing more than an unusual series of random coincidences. Even if there is a real pattern, more often than not the pattern will be discovered by other investors, and the more people who trade on the basis of any given pattern, the less profit it will generate until it is arbitraged all the way to zero. This is how markets evolve. What worked best in one bull market is unlikely to work in the next. What protected you from the last bear market is unlikely to protect you from the next. In one three-year period, I witnessed more than one hundred professionally managed funds launch to exploit a pattern that suddenly ceased to exist soon after the funds were launched. All but a handful of these funds were gone within three years.

In the early half of the 2000s, I was a quantitative analyst for a global hedge fund that employed computer algorithms to pick stocks in various markets. I spent four years of my life writing instructions to a computer to calculate the results of thousands of stock-picking methods. Every night, these instructions were sent to a bank of sixteen computers that were all very advanced at the time. Then every morning I arrived to work with pages of analysis waiting for me, all automatically sorted by risk-adjusted returns. We found all kinds of anomalies, and the fund was very successful, rising from a humble $200 million in assets at the beginning to more than $1 billion within a very short period of time. The most important lesson I learned from all this work, however, was that no strategy ever works for more than a few years at a time before it is arbitraged away.

Whenever you see a book, website, or magazine article suggesting that some particular investment strategy is back-tested, the first thing you should check is how far back the back-test really goes. Typically, you will see systems that have been tested for a period of three to four years, sometimes even as many as seven. These are the kinds of strategies that will blow up in your face the minute you invest your own money in them. The models are what statisticians call "overfitted" to a specific set of circumstances. As long as those circumstances prevail, the model performs spectacularly. As soon as the circumstances change, the model blows up. A very simple example of this would be a model that chose stocks with little or no profit and persistently rising share prices. Such a model would have generated extraordinary returns throughout the late 1990s but could easily have lost 90 percent or more of its assets as soon as the technology bubble burst.

Proponents of systems based on such short histories will usually argue that something or other was different "back then" and that because of such differences, back-testing of any prior periods would be counterproductive. But unless you are more than eighty years old, you can expect to be investing for more than another twenty years.

If you are just getting started, you might be investing for another sixty years. Do you really expect the next sixty years to be anything like the most recent seven years?

The point of studying long histories of prices is not to prove the future will be like the 1950s or the 1930s or any other specific period in history. The point is the one and only thing that is constant is change. It is my view that a good strategy works more because of its ability to capitalize on these changes rather than its ability to recognize and exploit persistent patterns. The farther back in history we peer, the more likely we are to find how these changes materialize and how to recognize them. Generally speaking, the less time involved in the study, the more likely it is that the model is overfitted.

Occasionally you will see systems that were tested over a period of fifteen or even twenty-five years, and these are likely to be more interesting, at least for educational purposes, but you need to be even more careful with them. Twenty-five years may seem like a long time. You might think that any patterns that were persistent for twenty-five years would have to be fairly reliable. But you would be as wrong about this as you could possibly be. Just twenty-five years ago, interest rates on a ten-year government bond were near their all-time peak of 14.94 percent, and since then the yield has fallen almost in a straight line to where they stand today at about 2 percent. There is no possibility that the next twenty-five years will resemble the past twenty-five years because yields cannot ever again drop to 2 percent from 15 percent, unless of course they go back up to 15 percent first. In many ways, these intermediate-term studies are even more dangerous because they really give the impression of being thorough and robust when in fact they cover a period of time that is unlike anything anyone alive has ever experienced or is likely to experience again.

Some historians have called the highly inflationary period that spanned the 1960s through the early 1980s the Twentieth Century Wave. They've called it that because in all of recorded human history, there were only a few others like it, with no two of them occurring in the same century.

Think about this: These waves have occurred before in the past, but no human being has ever experienced more than one in his or her lifetime. Yet this is the experience that drives the most fundamental beliefs about investing that almost all standard investment strategies are based on today. The last time inflation exploded, so did the money supply. One of the most influential economists in America wrote in 1963, "Inflation is always and everywhere a monetary phenomenon" (Friedman 1963). The consensus liked this explanation and chose to see a pattern that, as it turns out, does not actually exist. The money supply has exploded many times before in many different countries and has coincided with runaway inflation only about half the time. The result is that forty years later, many models based loosely on Friedman's theory blew up in our faces.

The system I'm going to show you was back-tested with data that goes all the way back to 1874. The model conveniently ignores a lot of seemingly important events that turn out to have been specific to their time and not indicative of any important long-term patterns, yet the model catches all the major turning points in market history.

Foresight

Back-tests, no matter how long or short, introduce another problem that is not present with real-time results. If we go back through history and mark each market peak and trough, then of course we will come up with a model that invests heavily at the bottom and lightly at the top of each cycle. Of course the returns will look spectacular. Such a model, in itself, would not be very useful at all because it would have us taking action in 1890 on the basis of information that wasn't available until 1990!

For example, one of the methodologies used very frequently in back-tests is valuation. The idea is to sell when valuations are high and buy when valuations are low. Say the average P/E ratio in the US equity market between 1870 and 2010 was 16 times (16x) historical earnings. If you decided to sell every time the market was 20x and to buy every time the market was 12x, you would have done pretty well throughout the period, but how would you have known in 1880 that the average P/E was 16x? Back then, the average was only 12x. Based on the same theory, the data available to you then would have led you to take very different actions, probably with much weaker results.

The only way to solve this problem is to leave some of the historical data out of the sample you use to create the model. First, you build the model using only a partial data set. You test various parameters and scenarios to ensure the model is robust within this smaller sample. Then you test it again on the out-of-sample data. Since none of the data from this out-of-sample set had any influence on the model, theoretically you have verified that the model does not suffer from hindsight.

Unfortunately, many modelers cheat on this technique by providing only superficial out-of-sample tests. If, for example, you have seven years of in-sample data and two years of out-of-sample data, the likelihood that those two years are really part of a different sample is very low. The stock and bond models in this book use an in-sample data set from 1870 through 2002 and an out-of-sample data set from 2003 to 2012. The out-of-sample data set is eleven years long, which makes it longer than most in-sample tests. And as any student of the market knows, the past eleven years were nothing like any previous decade, so there is virtually no possibility that the two data sets were part of the same set.

Of course, if you create a model that works well in sample but fails out of sample, the only thing to do is to go back to the drawing board. But if you go back to the drawing board, say one hundred times, before you arrive at a model that works out of sample, your out-of-sample data isn't really out of sample anymore. The model in this book was only tested on the out-of-sample data once, and it worked satisfactorily the first time. There was never a reason to go back to the drawing board.

One can never be 100 percent certain about anything when investing. There is one other way in which hindsight could have crept into this model. Even though the model did not use data from the out-of-sample set to make any of its calculations, as a researcher, I was certainly aware of the history of the past eleven years. It is always possible that my thinking could have been influenced by this knowledge in ways that are not conducive to good forecasting. I have endeavored to provide all the information needed in this book to anyone who wants to test this hypothesis, but I believe it will be hard to prove.

Leverage

The most important reason so many market-timing systems fail to add any value is that they set themselves up for failure before they even make a single market call. Typically, a model is either bullish, in which case the recommended position is 100 percent in the market, or bearish, in which case the recommended position is 100 percent in cash. Our model identifies six different conditions, each with a different risk-reward profile, so it is capable of much finer distinctions than most, but it still must solve a problem faced by all models. If your most bullish position is 100 percent invested, you can never outperform a rising market. Your best hope when you make a correct bullish call is to keep even with the market, yet every wrong call from the model will cause you to underperform. The only time you can outperform is when you make a correct bearish call.

Historically, the US stock market has spent about as many months going up as it has spent going down, so with a typical timing system, you have an opportunity to underperform the market all the time but an opportunity to outperform only half the time. These are very difficult odds to beat.

Let's say, for example, that you have a model that is correct 60 percent of the time on both its bullish and bearish calls. In this case, you would perform in line with the market 30 percent of the time, outperform 30 percent of the time, and underperform 40 percent of the time. That is a losing formula already, but in addition, every time you trade you create extra transaction costs, and every time you trade profitably, whether you outperform or not, you create an additional taxation drag on your returns, especially if you trade more than once a year. That is because short-term transactions with durations of less than one year are generally taxed at a higher rate. To overcome these hurdles, your model has to be correct at least 75 percent of the time. This is a rate of accuracy that turns out to be extraordinarily difficult to achieve.

There is one and only one way to overcome this obstacle, and it is surprising how few advisors ever figure this out: you must use leverage. Most advisors will never recommend leverage, and many will flat-out refuse to let you use leverage in accounts they control. They are too afraid of getting sued, and that's a rational fear because if they use leverage without a sound and statistically verified trading model, they can easily be found guilty of being imprudent.

Leverage provides a very simple and elegant solution to an otherwise impossible problem. Once you ensure that your correct bullish calls can outperform the market as easily as correct bearish calls, the hurdle rate is automatically lowered to about 55 percent. The reason it is not lowered to 51 percent is that you will have to pay interest on the amount of money you borrow from your broker. At this writing, discount brokers typically charge 8 percent per year. Later, I'll talk a little bit about how to lower this rate, but for the time being let's say you have a $10,000 position, take out a margin loan from your broker at 8 percent, and increase your position to $15,000 on our moderately bullish signal. Average returns on trades at this signal are 20.9 percent annually, so at the end of an average year, you would have $18,147.46. If you then pay back the $5,000 loan plus $400 in interest, you're left with $12,747.46—a 27.5 percent return, which still easily beats the market by a handy 6.5 percent.

If you increased the position to $20,000 on our most bullish signal, the average expected one-year return would be 25.3 percent. So on an average year, you would end up with $25,068.03, with which you would pay back the $10,000 loan plus $800 in interest and be left with $14,268.03. This would be a gain of 42.7 percent, which would beat the market by 17.3 percent.

Obviously, leverage is a double-edged sword, and just as it is capable of magnifying your gains, it can magnify losses. As long as you have a strategy and do not use leverage indiscriminately, it can reduce your risk. In back-tests dating all the way back to 1881, this model has recommended the use of moderate leverage only 25 percent of the time, and maximum leverage has been applied only 4 percent of the time.

Has it proved prudent to use leverage during the times the model recommended doing so? Absolutely. When using leverage, the maximum drawdown becomes a more important consideration than the average return. It won't do you much good to have an average return of 20 percent over the long run if on the very first attempt you get wiped out and don't have any capital to apply when the second signal comes around.

We are not going to let that happen. To ascertain the actual risk, I measured the cumulative return of each leveraged trade signaled by the model dating back to 1915. Of the twenty-four occasions moderate leverage was used for more than two consecutive months, the stock market outperformed inflation during twenty and underperformed only four times. The maximum drawdown of the market during any of these losing trades was 7 percent. Of the eight occasions when maximum leverage was recommended, five were positive in real terms, and only three were negative, with the maximum drawdown only 4 percent. This represents less risk and significantly more potential gain than what most people are exposed to in their homes, yet they feel perfectly comfortable having five to eight times as much leverage on their homes as they have on stocks.

Stocks have a very special advantage over real estate. Gaining leverage to the stock market does not require you to borrow money. When your objective is to double your exposure to the equity market, you can buy options for only pennies on the dollar, you can buy a basket of very highly leveraged stocks, or you can borrow money. I'll show you how to do this in a moment, but the important point is that as long as you only use moderate leverage when it is called for in a rigorously back-tested model such as the one described in this book, all of these methods are easy to execute and reasonably safe to use.

The option strategy is by far the most efficient. To gain $50,000 of exposure to the stock market using options at prices that prevailed at the time of this writing, you need only $6,078 in cash. This investment will give you the right to participate in any stock market rally as if you owned $50,000 worth of equity, but the most you can possibly lose is $6,078 plus commissions, which will probably be about $9. In the best-case scenario, as recorded by the historical track record of our model, you could gain almost $87,000 in profit. The efficiency of this strategy is demonstrated by a best-case to worst-case ratio of more than 14x, which simply means that for every additional unit of risk you take on, you get fourteen units of opportunity. Anytime this ratio is more than 3:1, you have a system that can be very profitable and worth taking advantage of if you can.

	Risk/Reward Comparison of Various Leverage Strategies							
Strategy	Cost of Additional Position	Transaction Cost	Interest Cost	Average Profit	Worst Case	Best Case	Worst Case x3	Best / Worst
Leverage	50,000	508	6,333	16,358.67	(13,941.33)	88,058.67	(28,141.33)	6.3
Beta	12,727	334	-	22,866.00	(7,434.00)	94,566.00	(12,726.50)	12.7
Options	6,078	310	-	17,144.00	(6,078.00)	86,857.00	(6,078.00)	14.3

Table 1: Options are the lowest cost, lowest risk way to gain leverage when bullish market conditions prevail.

Option strategies can seem daunting for beginning investors, but this is usually because most of the beginning textbooks try to teach you a lot of theory that requires an advanced degree in mathematics to begin to understand. You don't need to worry about any of that stuff because you are only going to be using one kind of option for one kind of purpose. I'm just going to go right ahead and show you exactly how to place an order, and you will see how easy it is to do.

In the order window for almost any online broker, there is a place to type in the underlying ticker symbol, in this case, SPY. There will be a place to choose between stocks or options. Choose "Options."

Once you choose "Options," you may be asked to choose from a variety of very complicated option strategies, none of which you need to pay any attention to. Just choose "Calls."

The next thing to do is choose the expiration. An option is a contract that gives you the option—but not the obligation—to buy the underlying securities at a specified price. All contracts expire. Shorter-term contracts provide greater leverage but are more likely to expire worthless. I recommend purchasing contracts that expire more than 365 days in the future to take advantage of the long-term capital gains tax rates if possible. The next choice is the strike price. Just choose a price that is closest to the current share price. This will usually be the most active option and the one that is priced the most efficiently. If you go very far away from the current price, you will suddenly be swimming in very deep water infested with very large sharks. You just don't need to go there. As long as you keep the strike price close to the current price and stick to options on index ETFs, you can get your options at a reasonable price.

Next you need to choose the quantity of contracts. For now, all you need to know is that you get exposure to one hundred shares with one contract. So if you want exposure to six hundred shares, you need to buy six contracts. I will show you how to know what exposure you want just a little bit later.

Next is the order type. Never buy an option at the market price. There are too many professional traders waiting to take advantage of you if you place a market order. Always place limit orders and wait patiently to get your price. Most online brokers will show you an indication of the bid, mid, and ask prices. The bid is the highest price at which anyone is currently willing to purchase the options, and the ask is the lowest price at which anyone is currently willing to sell.

Typically, for a one-year at-the-money option in a well-traded market index ETF, the ask price is only a percentage or two higher than the bid price, but you shouldn't need to pay the asking price. For one, we are never going to be buying options when we don't already have a 100 percent exposure to the market. There is no reason to hurry because even if the market rushes higher, you are at least fully invested already. Be patient and place an order for a limit price at or below the mid price. Option prices are usually volatile enough that you will almost always get your price eventually. If not, you can change your limit price the next day.

The only other thing you need to know is how many option contracts you need to get the exposure you want, and to calculate this, you only need one additional concept. This concept is called *delta*. Mathematicians often use the word *delta* to represent change, as the Greek letter delta is the first letter in the word διαφορά (pronounced *diaphorá*), meaning "difference." In options terminology, delta is the measure of how the option price changes in relation to the stock price. The delta on any call option will fall between 0 and 1. An option with a high delta will change more than an option with a low delta.

The closer the strike price is to the underlying stock price, and the closer the expiration date is to the preset, the higher the delta will be. If you buy an option with a strike price near the current price and an expiration more than one year out, the delta will typically be about 0.5, which means a single contract will move about 50 percent as much as the equivalent underlying shares would move. You need to buy two options to get full exposure to one hundred shares of any given stock if the delta is 0.5.

So the formula you need to use is as follows: the amount of exposure needed ÷ price of the Index ETF ÷ 100 ÷ delta = number of contracts needed.

If you need $50,000 of exposure, the price of the ETF is $163, and the delta of the option is 0.5, you need six options because $50,000 ÷ $163 = 306 shares. Round this off to 300. Then 300 shares ÷ 100 = three contracts, but divide this by the delta of 0.5 and you get six contracts.

You can easily find the delta of any option by going to the menu on the CBOE options calculator (http://www.cboe.com/). Choose "Tools" and then choose "Options Calculator." Type in the symbol of the underlying stock (in this case type *SPY*) and click "Go!" Type in the price of the SPY and the strike of the option you wish to purchase. Then choose the expiration date and click "Calculate."

The CBOE options calculator will calculate the fair price and the delta. All you need is the delta. The fair price might be available in the market, but often it is not. There are many ways to calculate the fair value of an option, and the CBOE's method is not always right. If you place a limit order inside the bid-ask spread, you will usually get a reasonable price.

Our strategy is long-term, so the exact price you pay for the option, as long as it is within reason, is not going to make a major difference to your outcome. Just understand that you are usually going to get stuck paying a premium price for your options and that this premium is just a price you pay for the privilege of owning the options. The premium you pay will vary with the liquidity and volatility of the underlying stock, which is why I only recommend buying long-term options on index ETFs. The options on these ETFs are very heavily traded and very liquid, so the premiums are very tiny compared to what you would pay on individual securities. And by purchasing the longer-dated options, you pay fewer premiums and probably less tax on your profits.

Selling the Market Short

Many financial advisors will tell you to never short the market. They should all be fired. The fact is that there are times when shorting the market has the lowest risk-reward ratio of any asset class in the world, and in these times it is actually the investors who don't sell short who take on too much risk.

The main reason most financial advisors don't want you to short the market is that they don't know how to do it themselves. No financial advisor training program I am aware of in the United States teaches advisors how to short stocks.

One of the reasons training doesn't exist is that shorting the market is not something large reputable firms want to promote because of the idea that it is somehow immoral. Short-sellers are seen by many to make money at others' expense, and these others are someone's clients. Here is a news flash: people who buy stocks low and sell them high are making money at someone else's expense.

There is no moral high ground in the stock market. It is a competitive arena in which there are always winners and losers. If I buy a stock at ten dollars from trader Joe and sell it to trader Jack at a price of $15, I make $5. There is no moral difference whatsoever between this transaction and one in which I first sell the stock to trader Jack at $15 and then buy it from trader Joe at $10. In both cases, I make money at both of their expenses because trader Joe could have sold directly to trader Jack at $12.50, and both would have been better off. For whatever reason, at the time that Joe wanted to sell, Jack wasn't there, so I made money because I was willing to trade with Jack at a time Joe was not and with Joe at a time Jack no longer held the shares. Regardless of whether I am long or short, there is no good guy and no bad guy involved. There are only winners and losers.

Another objection that is often raised about short-selling is that the most you can gain is 100 percent of your investment if the stock goes to zero, while the amount you can lose is infinite because there is no limit to how high the stock can go. I am still waiting for someone to show me an example of a stock that went to infinity, but this argument isn't relevant for our purposes because we are going to go short the same way we added leverage, namely by purchasing options. You cannot lose any more than what you invested in an option.

The only difference between using options to go short and options to go long is that instead of buying call options, we buy put options. Put options give you the right but not the obligation to sell the stock or index at a certain price. Continuing with our previous example of a portfolio with a policy exposure to equities of $100,000, you can get the same $50,000 of short exposure for a fraction of the cost of shorting the actual shares. In this case, at the time of this writing, put options were less expensive than calls, so you would have to pay $5,670 plus commissions. This still represents your maximum loss, while the expected average annualized gain would be about $13,000.

The argument for shorting the market is slightly less compelling than the argument for using leverage. You do not *need* to short the market to outperform when making a correct bearish call. Just underweight equities and you'll do better than the majority of investors. But what is the reason you buy equities in the first place? Is it not because you expect to make a capital gain when they go up in price? And on what do you base the assumption that they will go up in price? Isn't it that historically they have tended to do so in the long run? Or perhaps it is because you think you can buy assets at a price that is below the intrinsic value of their future earnings potential.

What would you do if I could show you an asset that historically tended to go down? You could simply ignore it and thus avoid losing money, but what if this was the only asset you could buy and it always went down? You could avoid it and be better off than everyone who owned it, but you would never increase your wealth. If it makes sense to invest in stocks because you think they will go up, it makes sense to short them if you think the price will go down.

Historically, when our model has rendered its most bearish signal, monthly returns have ranged between +1.5 percent and –4.5 percent in 95 percent of cases, with an average of –1.5 percent per month. The highest monthly return ever was 6 percent. The average annualized rate of return was –16.5 percent.

If you simply ignore the stock market and go into bonds, you are still taking a risk. It is always possible that bonds might also lose money. If you go into cash, you can still lose purchasing power if inflation exceeds the yield on cash. There is no possibility of avoiding risk entirely. The risk you take when going short in the market when the stock market model is at its most extreme negative position is no greater than the risk of holding bonds or cash. In fact, it's possibly a lot lower, and the returns are potentially much higher.

The only real questions are how much to short and how to do it. You don't ever need to be aggressive on the short side. If you are making a little money when everyone else is losing a lot of money, you are going to be the king of the hill. I recommend being short no more than 50 percent of your normal policy equity exposure. I will talk more about policy exposure later in this book, but for example, if you are forty years old and have a normal risk tolerance, you probably have a policy of holding 60 percent of your assets in equities. During extreme bearish signals, you would then want to be 30 percent short. While your policy would have resulted, on average, in a 10 percent decline, the tactical model would have enabled you to add 5 percent to your nest egg. This is a 15 percent outperformance with only half the amount of gross exposure a buy-and-hold strategy would entail.

CHAPTER 3

A Primer on Tactics and Strategy

The conventional methodology for determining a long-term asset allocation strategy, or investment policy, for an individual is to subtract your age from one hundred to get your appropriate stock weighting. If you are thirty, equities would be 70 percent of your portfolio. If you are fifty, equities would be 50 percent of your portfolio. If you are seventy, equities should take up no more than 30 percent of your portfolio.

The advantage of this approach is that it is incredibly simple and easy to follow, and it is based on the intuitively sound principle that the older you get, the less time you have to make up losses. The disadvantages are that it is based on incomplete and outdated information and forces you to accept very suboptimal results. It is incapable of adapting to changes in circumstances.

To develop a superior approach, the first thing we need to do is eliminate all of the inaccurate assumptions inherent in this approach and develop a superior static model, which we will call our strategic, or policy, model. Then we can use this policy model as a baseline from which to build a more robust tactical model, which we will use to periodically adjust the weightings of each asset class to capitalize on changes in our assessment of the potential risks and rewards of each asset class.

Establishing a Baseline

The conventional way of explaining the age-based approach to asset allocation is that the closer you get to retirement, the less time you have to recover any losses. Actually, this isn't exactly true, given the length of time people live beyond retirement these days. A better way to understand the sensitivity to age is to use the net present value of your future savings as an asset class. At the beginning of your career, the net present value of your future savings is 100 percent of your net worth. When you save 10 percent of your first year's salary—no matter how much or how little you make—the value of your future savings is still probably at least 98 percent of your net worth. If you lose 100 percent of that investment, the total loss is still no more of a loss than 2 percent of your total net worth. It is not the time you have to recover that is important. The important fact is that relative to the net present value of your lifetime savings, the amount of money you've lost is still trivial.

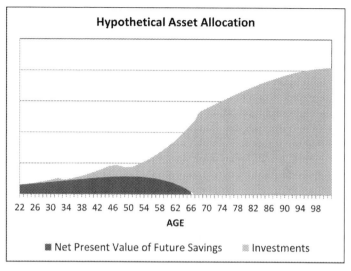

Chart 4: During the first twenty-five years of your investing career, the present value of future income from your career will far outweigh any investment considerations.

Unfortunately, the net present value of your lifetime earnings is no longer as risk-free as it used to be. People get laid off or forced into early retirement with increasing frequency. They get robbed of their pensions by unscrupulous and incompetent managers. Industries decline, and experienced workers have to change careers, often requiring greatly reduced incomes. Even with no change in income, the net present value of everyone's future savings is lower because we have to adjust it for the very heightened possibility that you will not earn as much over your lifetime as you expect. And as a result of this much lower net present value of future savings, any losses experienced in your portfolio are more significant than conventional asset allocation models allow for.

An equally serious problem is that the rule of thumb is based on assumptions about equity and bond returns that simply aren't valid. During the period between 1970 and 2012, bonds actually outperformed stocks and were less volatile. During this period, the higher your exposure to equities, the lower your returns were and the higher your volatility. That's exactly the opposite result than the conventional model returns. As we've already discussed, there is no reason to believe that what happened during the past forty years will be repeated in the next forty years, but there is ample reason to be concerned that the static model is based on invalid assumptions.

A third problem with the static model is that both bonds and stocks can exhibit negative returns simultaneously for extended periods of time. The correlation between bond and stock returns is low, but it is not perfectly inverse. The static two asset class model can be improved significantly by including gold and cash as asset classes. A couple of interesting points can be made about table 2, which lists a large number of possible variations in fixed weightings and their return characteristics. The first is that incremental increases and decreases in equity exposure have a completely random effect on total return but in general reduce risk-adjusted return. The question you should be asking then, regardless of one's age, is why one should take a higher level of risk if there is no significant compensation in expected return. There isn't a very good reason.

The final nail in the coffin is one you could easily figure out without any of the data. The idea of reducing risk by a fixed increment for every increase in age is just far too simpleminded. The net present value of your future savings doesn't fall off at a fixed rate.

In the first twenty years of your career, even if you save 10 percent of your income every month and invest very astutely, the net present value of your future savings will still exceed 50 percent of your real net worth. The volatility of your investments will still not have a significant effect on your total net worth. Sometime during your fifth decade, however, the net present value of your future savings will start to decline more rapidly, and the value of your investments will start to increase dramatically.

Very suddenly you won't be able to take as much risk as you are accustomed to taking without it hurting you fairly severely. The two decades between the time you turn fifty and the time you turn seventy is the period when people get hurt the most because they often don't realize how much more sensitive their net worth has become to changes in the value of their portfolios.

In my view, the conventional wisdom of cutting back 10 percent of your equity exposure for each decade of your age is probably not conservative enough. In table 2, I show the back-tested results of the tactical allocation models based on various age-related policy weighting assumptions. Notice that the maximum one-month drawdown for an 80/10/10 policy is –12.7 percent, and as the equity exposure is reduced in each decade, the maximum drawdown continues to recede until it is just 2.1 percent. Now look at the line that shows this drawdown as a percent of total net worth when the net present value of future savings is included. In the first decade, that 12.7 percent drawdown is converted to a mere 1.8 percent. In no scenario does the maximum drawdown ever exceed 6 percent.

In fact, to keep the maximum drawdown below 6 percent, we needed to accelerate the reduction in equity exposure at age fifty. Instead of dropping it to 50 percent, I dropped it to 40 percent. I also set the maximum exposure to TLT and GLD at 20 percent and tilted exposure toward TLT in later decades while rapidly increasing the policy exposure to money market funds from the initial point of 0 percent all the way up to 60 percent.

You do not need to follow the age-based policies precisely. Everyone is different. If you are more tolerant of risk, you might benefit from following the model for someone ten years younger than your actual age. If you are less tolerant of risk, you may wish to follow the model for someone ten years your senior.

Effect on Risk and Reward of Age-Based Adjustments to Portfolio Strategy								
Approximate Age	20	30	40	50	60	70	80	90
Investment Portfolio Policy Weighting								
SPY	80%	70%	60%	40%	30%	20%	10%	0%
TLT	10%	15%	20%	20%	30%	30%	30%	30%
GLD	10%	15%	20%	20%	10%	10%	10%	10%
MMKT	0%	0%	0%	20%	30%	40%	50%	60%
Total	100%	100%	100%	100%	100%	100%	100%	100%
Back Tested Results 1971 - 2012								
Worst Month	-12.7%	12.2%	11.7%	-9.3%	-5.9%	-4.4%	-3.0%	-2.1%
Best Month	12.6%	11.6%	10.5%	9.0%	5.7%	5.2%	4.8%	4.4%
Avg Month	0.93%	0.91%	0.89%	0.78%	0.70%	0.64%	0.55%	0.54%
Standard Deviation	2.8%	2.5%	2.3%	1.8%	1.3%	1.0%	0.7%	0.6%
Sharpe Ratio	33.4%	35.7%	37.9%	44.3%	54.0%	63.8%	83.1%	82.5%
Total Net Worth Policy Weighting								
Future Savings	92%	85%	60%	41%	10%	0%	0%	0%
Investments	8%	15%	40%	59%	90%	100%	100%	100%
Weighted Return								
Worst Month	-1.0%	-1.8%	-4.7%	-5.5%	-5.3%	-4.4%	-3.0%	-2.1%
Best Month	1.0%	1.7%	4.2%	5.3%	5.1%	5.2%	4.8%	4.4%
Avg Month	0.1%	0.1%	0.4%	0.5%	0.6%	0.6%	0.6%	0.5%
Standard deviation	0.2%	0.4%	0.9%	1.1%	1.2%	1.0%	0.7%	0.6%
Sharpe Ratio	33.4%	35.7%	37.9%	43.3%	54.0%	63.8%	78.6%	82.5%

Table 2: Asset allocations optimized to minimize the downside risk to total net worth including the present value of future savings.

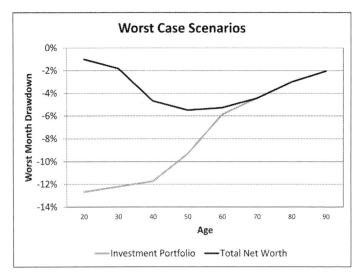

Chart 5: Worst-case scenarios are greatly reduced when considering the net present value of future savings.

Blending Tactics with Strategy

The rest of this book will consist of chapters on each asset class and explain how you can tactically increase or decrease the relative weighting above or below the policy weighting to take advantage of changes in the risk assessment. Regardless of the policy weightings you choose, I can show you a way to consistently exceed the expected returns of that policy by about 2–3 percent annually without increasing your risk. While 2–3 percent may seem trivial, over a thirty-year investing career, it is enough to double the size of the nest egg you would have ended up with using the static approach.

I use a separate model each for equities, bonds, and gold. Whenever the sum of recommended weightings from each of these three models is less than 100 percent, the difference is transferred to a bond fund if the bond model is positive or a money market fund if the bond market model is negative.

The only caveat is that I will never let the bond market allocation get larger than the policy allocation for equities. For example, if the policy model calls for a stock weighting of 60 percent, the bond allocation can never exceed 60 percent even if the stock and gold models are both negative. In such a case, bonds would first receive their 20 percent policy allocation because the bond market is positive, plus up to 40 percent additional allocation because of negative allocations from equities and gold. The remaining 40 percent would be placed in a money market fund.

Whenever the total allocation from each model is more than 100 percent, I will show the cash value as a negative number, indicating the percent of assets that are borrowed. This can never exceed 60 percent in practice because the highest policy weighting for equities is 60 percent and the highest tactical weighting is 200 percent of policy. Leverage is never used for bonds or gold, so the highest allocation these assets can receive in combination is 40 percent.

Thus, the maximum active allocation is 120 percent to equities and 40 percent to gold and bonds. Total effective borrowing would be 60 percent. In all probability, you will not ever actually borrow this money; rather, you will simulate such borrowing either by purchasing more volatile equities or by purchasing options. Either will give you the same potential increase in return with far less risk. I'll show you exactly how easy this is in the next chapter.

CHAPTER 4

Stocks

The basis of most financial-planning advice on stock market investing is one of the most outrageous lies in finance. It is based on the observation that the long-term return on stocks has averaged 10 percent and that although there are minor deviations from year to year, no one has ever been able to time these deviations effectively. Therefore, we are told that stocks always outperform in the long run, that good investors stay the course, and that timing the market is the worst thing you can do to your wealth.

The truth is not so elegant. Real returns from the stock market have averaged less than 4 percent over the past 130 years. Since you are taxed on the nominal returns, the after-tax returns are only about 3 percent, and even this kind of return is extraordinarily inconsistent and unreliable. In the five best ten-year runs, the market averaged more than 240 percent, while the five worst ten-year runs lost more than 40 percent on average. In fact, the worst thing you can do to your wealth is to *not* time the market. If you had all your money in the stock market at the beginning of one of these bad spells and you had no other source of income, you would be in a lot of pain.

What's amazing is that these stay-the-course monkeys failed to notice that every single one of the best decades was preceded by a valuation measure that was way below average, while the worst were all preceded by measures that were well above average. The measure of valuation is neither easy nor straightforward, and this is the main reason that even professional investors are often doubtful about its merits. Valuation is not the only thing that matters, but it is way ahead of everything else in importance.

Valuation matters enough to ruin the lives of those who do not pay attention. More importantly, it is possible for mere mortals to make long-term forecasts based on very simple and extremely accurate information that is readily available to everyone. You do not need to have an advanced degree from an Ivy League institution, and you do not need to pay millions of commission dollars to gain access to the information.

Valuation Matters

At the top of every market cycle in the past thirty years, I've seen at least one extremely intelligent Wall Street strategist explain very eloquently why equities must go higher and why I'd be a fool not to increase my equities position. There is never any readily visible flaw in their arguments. Wall Street strategists are among the most highly paid snake-oil salesmen and saleswomen the world have ever known, and yet at almost every turning point they are consistently and horribly wrong. You see, they do not get paid to be right. They get paid to paint a rosy scenario, and they are paid extremely well.

A standard technique for selling anything is to make it seem like a bargain you cannot afford to miss. For something that is actually not a bargain, any competent snake-oil salesman or saleswoman can readily fake it with one of two standard methodologies:

1. Compare it to something that is even more outrageously priced.
2. Just lie about what is inside the bottle.

Let's look at some examples of the first methodology. You might compare a forty-dollar bottle of wine to a two-hundred-dollar bottle of wine, and since they're in bottles that are the same size, naturally people who do not know very much about wine will gravitate to the forty-dollar bottle. You may be thinking, *Why a two-hundred-dollar bottle? Wouldn't a fifty-dollar bottle suffice?* The answer is no, it wouldn't. A fifty-dollar bottle would invite educated comparisons. You would end up being forced to give the consumer his or her money's worth. With a two-hundred-dollar bottle, few customers will be fooled into thinking they are getting the same exact content for an 80 percent discount. In a way, the retailer is pretending to be dumb by inviting an obviously invalid comparison. Instead, the consumer is more likely to decide that whatever the difference in quality is, it can't be worth $160. The ruse, however, is that the contents of the forty-dollar bottle is no different than that of a thirty-dollar bottle of wine that may or may not be on display. The ruse works because the consumer is tricked into thinking he or she has enough information to make an economically astute decision. The reality is that he or she has no useful information whatsoever.

For equities, the item of comparison is usually a bond. The standard measure of value for a stock is the price-to-earnings ratio, which is a massive oversimplification I will talk about later in this chapter, but for now it is a ratio that works for the purpose of this ruse. You are buying a share of the earnings in the company, so it makes sense to compare the price of the shares to the earnings you are buying.

The problem with this is that bonds don't have a P/E ratio, so we need to do a little math to make the bonds and the stocks comparable. To do this, analysts usually convert a P/E ratio into an earnings yield, which is simply the inverse of the P/E ratio. Instead of dividing P by E, divide E by P. Now both bonds and stocks have a yield, so it seems like they should be directly comparable. This simple valuation model is commonly known as the Fed Model because it was popularized by former Federal Reserve Chairman Alan Greenspan, but the actual model is much older than even Greenspan.

Intuitively, one wants to buy the asset with the highest yield. The reality, however, is that relative yield does not predict relative return. The scatter graph below, based on monthly data of the S&P 500 and ten-year treasuries, shows that the correlation between interest rates and earnings yields is statistically equivalent to zero.

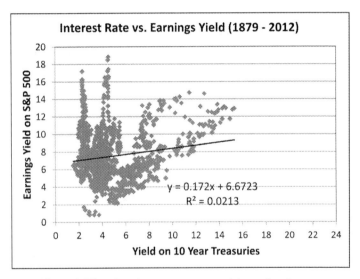

Chart 6: The idea that interest rates drive valuations on equities is a total myth. There is no correlation between interest rates and earnings yields on stocks.

If there was any relationship between earnings yields and bond yields, the dots on chart 5 would all line up along a common axis. If they were correlated, as the Fed Model implies, the line would slope upward. If they were inversely correlated (i.e., if stock yields went up when bond yields went down), the line would slope downward. But as you can see, there is no correlation. The dots are scattered randomly.

I hope you are skeptical of this graph. Intuitively, it is incorrect, and whenever you are presented with hard factual data that is intuitively incorrect, you should question it. When interest rates go down, the value of my house goes up because it costs less to pay the mortgage. It seems common sense that when interest rates go down, the cost of borrowing money used to buy assets goes down; therefore, the value of other assets must go up. The same should apply to equities. So how is it possible that the dots on this graph are scattered randomly?

Unfortunately, what appears to be common sense is nothing more than an illusion, even for houses. Interest rates are at an all-time low, and if you checked the value of your house recently, you know that it is not at an all-time high.

If we look at a linear chart in chart 6, based on the same data as in chart 5 our eyes see slightly more pattern. We can also see that stocks clearly yield much more than bonds now, and this drives most financial advisors crazy. They wonder aloud to anyone who will listen, "Why would you buy a bond if a stock yields more?"

As with the forty-dollar bottle of wine, the commonsense answer is wrong because we lack sufficient information. Before 1962, it was normal for stocks to yield more than bonds, but that was fifty years ago. To remember it, you'd have to be at least eighty years old today. Suffice it to say that most people alive today do not remember the period of history that is most like today.

The current differential between stocks and bonds is not exceptional by any measure. It is true that during the past thirty years or so, earnings yields seem to have been more correlated with bond yields than at any previous time, but is that because the markets have become more efficient, as many observers assume, or is there some more temporal reason that might not prove sustainable? Let us stop with the assuming and conduct a rigorous mathematical examination. Even during this later period, the level of interest rates explains only 50 percent of the level of the earnings yield. So using the bond yield to measure equity valuation even in the best of conditions is no better than tossing a coin.

But why? How is this possible? One possible explanation would be that low interest rates are less correlated with earnings yield than high interest rates, but this is only an important clue. It doesn't explain why low rates should be any different than high rates. It's not the full explanation.

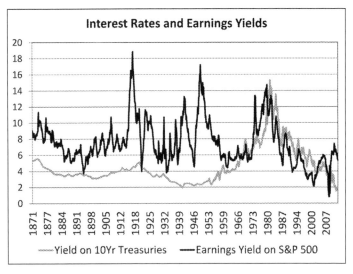

Chart 7: Low interest rates more often coincide with
high volatility rather than low earnings yields.

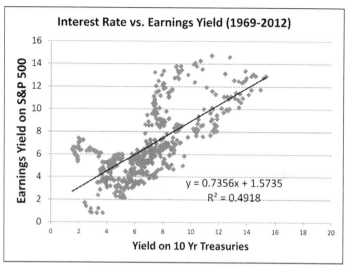

Chart 8: Even in recent decades, rates explain only about half of the total movement in earnings yields.

The answer is that interest rates do affect asset prices, but they are only one thing among many others that influence the price. Like all valuation models, this comparison of current yields is just a simplification of the discounted cash flow (DCF) model. The DCF model measures the value of all cash flows an asset is likely to generate over its lifetime and discounts them by an interest rate (known as the risk premium) to get the net present value. The disadvantage of the DCF model is that there are more variables in it and therefore more opportunities to be wrong. People don't like to use it for this reason, and they are always coming up with simplifications, but if you don't understand the DCF model, you won't understand what these simplifications are giving up in terms of accuracy.

The discounted present value for any asset can be expressed as DPV = FV/(d–g), where DPV is the discounted present value of the future cash flow (FV); FV is the nominal value of a cash flow amount in a future period; *g* is the growth rate; and *d* is the discount rate, which reflects both the cost of tying up capital and the risk premium associated with the possibility that the expected growth rate might not be achieved.

The Fed Model focuses exclusively on near-term earnings and the risk-free interest rate. It completely excludes two extremely important factors: the rate of future growth in earnings and the risk premium. The Fed Model can still work if either of these factors are constant or when they cancel each other out. It just so happens that they tend to cancel each other out when interest rates are high. In high-interest-rate environments, higher growth tends to be associated with higher risk, so these two factors often move in opposite directions, and indeed they cancel each other out. Not surprisingly, the Fed Model was popularized during a time when the two things it ignores were temporarily rendered unimportant.

Low-interest-rate environments are very different. The lower rates are caused by significantly lower growth expectations. Thus, lower rates occur during periods when earnings are weak and inconsistent, which is a cause for the risk premium to be higher and more volatile. This is why you can often see the earnings yield rising to much higher levels during low-interest-rate environments than it ever does during high-interest-rate environments.

So now that interest rates are about as low as at any other time in history, there is a greater risk that the risk premium itself will continually go into spasms of volatility, creating wild swings in share prices that are totally unrelated to either earnings or interest rates. A model that ignores this is likely to be wrong almost all of the time.

We also now have our first hard evidence of how important it is to study extremely long periods of history. Fluctuations in the rate of earnings growth and the discount rate were rendered unimportant for almost three decades. Anyone studying only those three decades would have been tempted to conclude that these two things never matter. This conclusion would defy common sense, and a longer-term study verifies that the past three decades were in fact abnormal aberrations that are unlikely to be sustained much longer.

The Only Earnings Measure You Need

The second, and by far the more damaging, way to make a product or service seem like a bargain when it really is not is to flat-out lie about what is inside the box. This is effectively what almost all sell-side strategists do for a living. They do not get paid to make stocks look unattractive. They do not get paid to be right.

Now we are ready to talk about the use of current earnings in the valuation of equities. This is the easiest and by far the most common method for distorting the truth about stocks. Stocks are a claim on *all* future earnings, of which the current earnings are only a very tiny fraction. In general, it is easy to get away with this because for most people, even professional Wall Street analysts and fund managers, having to worry about the entire future stream of earnings is just too complicated. Unfortunately, whenever you use a price-to-current-earnings ratio, you are making a substitution. You are substituting the easy to use but inaccurate current earnings for the complicated net present value of future earnings. Intuitively, future earnings should be somehow related to current earnings. You would think the best way for a company to have high earnings in one year is to have had high earnings the year before. If this were true, there would be little harm in making this kind of simplification.

The reality, however, is that corporate earnings are so cyclical that current earnings are actually inversely correlated to future earnings. When current earnings are high, future earnings are almost certain to be low, and when current earnings are depressed, future earnings are almost as certain to be higher. This formula can actually be used to explain 70 percent of the subsequent five-year growth in US corporate earnings. As of the time of this writing, current earnings were 5.2 percent of GDP— nearly an all-time high. There are no examples in history of earnings being this high and not declining over the subsequent five years.

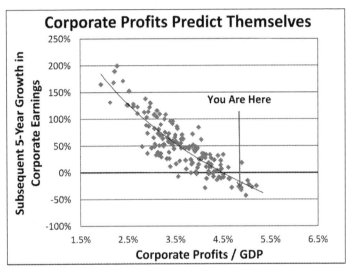

Chart 9: High corporate profits to GDP
ratios tend to lead to slow growth.

If we stretch this data out into a line graph and plug in the forecast, we see that the model is projecting the most aggressive decline in earnings since the data became available. A common criticism of this model is that it does not take into account the fact that during the period that is being modeled, foreign-earned income increased to 40 percent of total corporate profits at the end of the period from about 20 percent at the beginning of the period. This particular criticism doesn't work very well, however. Despite this increase in foreign earnings, the model accurately predicted the

2008–2009 decline in earnings. There is also no evidence whatsoever that the increase in foreign earnings has ever or could ever have any effect on the cyclical nature of earnings in general.

We should still be very careful not to place too much faith in the forecast made by this model. It is only based on a single factor, and the data available includes only a few recessions. The point here is not to prove that earnings will grow or decline but rather to know that in our search for a reliable substitute for future cash flows, current earnings are the worst possible choice.

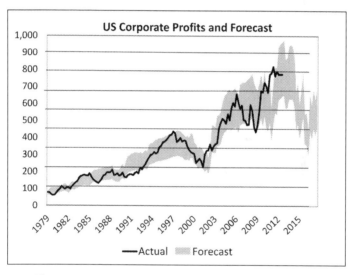

Chart 10: Corporate profits are not stable and shouldn't be relied on to bail you out of bad investments.

Why You Absolutely Must Time the Market

There are two possible methods statisticians use to normalize a series of data points that consistently revert to the mean. For a very long time, I used to rely on an exponential trend line, which was based on the observation that earnings had risen 2.2 percent annually for more than one hundred years. Then I met a strategist from one of the bulge-bracket brokers who used the same exact method, yet she had come to the opposite conclusion as I had about where stocks were headed. There was obviously something wrong with a methodology that, if applied consistently by two different people, could deliver two diametrically opposed conclusions at any given point in time.

I quickly discovered the first part of the problem. The bulge-bracket strategist was using nominal earnings. Whenever you are comparing prices at one time to prices at another, whether it be the price of stocks or the price of corn, using nominal prices is just dishonest. If you sell one hundred dollars of stock today, you cannot buy the same amount of goods or services with that cash that you could have bought after selling a stock for one hundred dollars in 1928. A long-term trend line over a nominal price series is simply not going to tell you anything meaningful.

In the process of reviewing this data, however, I noticed another problem. In this case, I was the one guilty of being dishonest, at least to myself, which is something all researchers are prone to if they do not exercise extreme discipline. The question I failed to ask was, "Why do earnings rise at 2.2 percent after inflation?" The obvious answer is that there is no good reason whatsoever. Just because earnings grew at that rate before does not qualify as a reason. Clearly, they have not grown at that rate consistently. There have been many periods when growth was much higher than this and many in which it was much lower. I did not have a valid theory upon which to base any viable prediction of future growth.

My 2.2 percent prediction was nothing more than the result I had observed by noting a randomly selected starting date and a randomly selected ending date and calculating the rate of growth based on the number of years between these two isolated incidents in time.

Unfortunately, a trend such as this, even when calculated over several decades, is extremely sensitive to the starting and ending points. If one started in 1891 and finished in 1945, the rate of growth drops to 0.7 percent. If one started in 1921 and ended in 1967, the rate rises to 2.9 percent. If one calculates from the earliest available date to the latest, the actual average growth rate is 1.8 percent. These differences may seem immaterial on an annual basis, but by 2013 the forecast generated by a rate of 2.9 percent is four times the forecast generated by a 0.7 percent rate. Even my use of a period that resulted in a conclusion of 2.2 percent was far enough off the mark that after ten years of using the data, I was starting to get unrealistic and very problematic readings from my model.

One can measure the mean over several different nonoverlapping periods to verify the persistence of the mean. If you get roughly the same answer in each period, you have found the true mean. As it turns out, 1.8 percent is a much more realistic appraisal of the true mean rate of earnings growth over inflation, but even with this rate, there is no obvious reason for it to persist. Without a valid reason, there is no valid means of making a forecast. All that exists is a historical artifact that may just as easily be a coincidence rather than a causal relationship.

It is plausible that survivorship bias accounts for a substantial portion of the persistency of inflation adjusted growth. The S&P Index Committee actively evaluates the index components every four to six weeks, and annual changes average about thirty-eight per year, with much higher numbers of replacements occurring during recessions. Clearly, the new members are more successful than the ones they replaced. Another very plausible contribution to the excess growth of earnings could be that the consumer price index measures price changes inaccurately or that it measures the wrong set of prices.

Whenever you drive investments from conclusions that are drawn on the basis of historical data without a verifiable cause, you are often taking far more risk than you could possibly realize. If I had been investing in 1945, I would not have known what the end-data point was in 2013, so I would not have known what the actual growth rate was going to be. If I had used the existing trend as my guide, without questioning it I would have exited the equity market by about 1948 and never touched equities ever again. This clearly would not have led to satisfactory results.

Fortunately, there is a work-around that enables us to use data that was available as early as 1881 and does not require us to unravel any mysteries of the universe. A much less ambitious way of normalizing earnings is to take a ten-year moving average of earnings. This is a long-enough average to include at least one peak and one trough in almost any cycle that has ever occurred but not so long that it fails to respond to secular changes in growth rates. Our hypothesis now is merely that earnings are cyclical, and whatever current earnings are now, they are more likely to move toward the historical mean than to move away from it. This is a sound hypothesis that economists have been observing since the invention of money. There is little agreement among economists about the causes. Many plausible theories are available, and the one thing that all agree on is that the cycles exist.

The only theoretical concern regarding the use of a moving average is that if the period used is too long, it may significantly lag the actual earnings, and this may lead to underestimation, especially during the early stages of a recovery when earnings are rising rapidly and the moving average is still being dragged downward by historical data that is no longer relevant. This is a legitimate theoretical concern, but as the graph below demonstrates, it is really not a problem in practice. The ten-year moving average tracks the actual earnings much more closely than the long-term trend line and has never in practice lagged actual earnings by enough to be a serious problem.

If the price of the S&P 500 is now divided by this measure of normalized earnings, the result is a measure of value that is commonly referred to as the Shiller P/E ratio in reference to Nobel Prize winner Robert Shiller, who himself uses the term CAPE for cyclically adjusted price-to-earnings ratio.

From 1981 through 2003, the Shiller P/E averaged 16x. During this time, the total return on stock market indexes averaged 3.3 percent plus inflation, but if you had added to holdings whenever the Shiller P/E was below 9x and reduced holdings whenever it was above 23x, you could have increased the total return to 4.8 percent plus inflation. This may not sound like much of an improvement, but if one applies this model at the beginning of one's investing career, say at the age of twenty-five, it is almost enough to double the actual results by the time you are ready to retire at age sixty-five. (Technically, at this rate you would actually double the results by age seventy-three.)

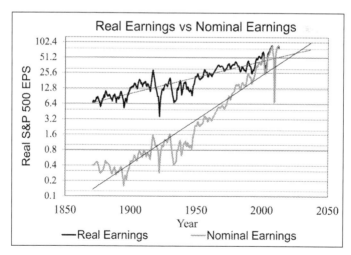

Chart 11: The trend is your friend, but only if you choose the right one. Be careful to draw the trend line from the middle of one cycle to the middle of another. Many sell-side analysts draw the trend from trough to peak and generate equally strong historical back-tests, but they are based on totally unsustainable assumptions.

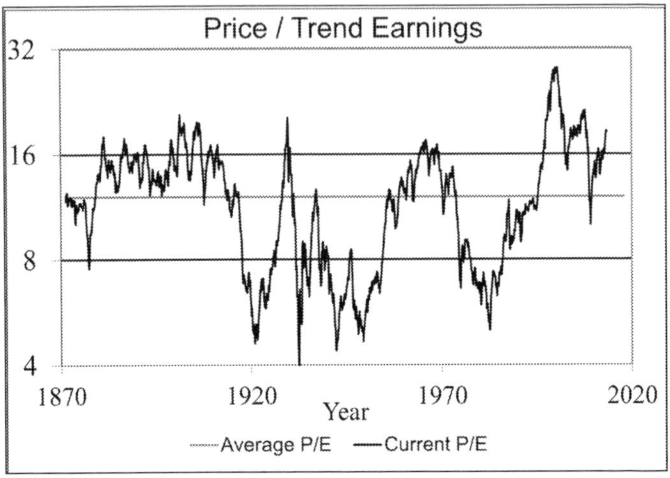

Chart 12: Corporate profits have risen at a rate of 3.5 percent plus inflation consistently for as long as data has been available, and stock prices rarely stray too far from the same trend line.

Beating the Stock Market

The Shiller P/E is far from perfect. You would still suffer from very long and frustrating periods of loss. By long periods, I mean that on occasion you would spend more than a decade without making any money. It would be extremely difficult for most human beings to go through such periods and feel as if they were accomplishing anything. The temptation to abandon the system and try something new under such pressure is too great for most people, and that is why so few people use the Shiller P/E even though it is widely available and very well-known.

Looking at the chart of the Shiller P/E, though, a couple of observations make it possible to develop an improvement. To create simple statistical models and form truly valid forecasts, the time series being forecasted needs to have two characteristics: it must be mean reverting, and it must be stationary. Mean reverting means that the extreme data points, whether they are high or low, must be unsustainable, and whenever they are reached, the subsequent data points must have a strong tendency to move back toward the mean. Stationary indicates that the mean and the extremes do not move around. Their values are relatively constant.

The Shiller P/E is mean reverting, but it is not stationary. No two peaks or troughs have ever been recorded at exactly the same level, and the speed at which the data reverts to the mean is also never the same. If you try to use this data to pinpoint an exact price at which the market will peak or trough, you will fail. This is probably the most frustrating phenomenon any value investor ever faces. It is the reason that many hardened value investors fail and the reason that many investors dismiss value altogether. You cannot set a target price based on valuation because the stock will almost never stop at your target.

I have developed a work-around for this problem that, as far as I am aware, makes my approach to asset allocation unique. I developed this technique from years of observing cyclical companies and learning to call the tops and bottoms in these hyperactive stocks. I noticed that if you divide the P/E chart into segments with the largest part in the middle representing a fair value range and the subsequently smaller bands on either side representing slightly and greatly overvalued levels, a very counterintuitive thing happens. The stock, or in this case the index, usually moves through the slightly overvalued phase twice: once on the way up and once on the way down. It may or may not ever enter the extremely overvalued phase. The same is true on the undervaluation side. From a pure valuation methodology, there is no way to distinguish between the phase in which the stock moves upward through the overvalued territory and the second phase in which it moves downward through the overvaluation territory. To a computer measuring value, both of these phases are identical, but if you own the stock, your results are exactly the opposite in each phase.

I've introduced a very simple solution to this problem that allows you to mechanically determine whether the market is moving upward or downward through any particular valuation phase. Typically, when stocks move upward from slightly overvalued to extremely overvalued, the current price will consistently be higher than the long-term moving average, and when it is moving downward from extreme overvaluation to just plain overvaluation, it will be priced below the moving average.

The way the combined model works is it starts with a valuation model that weights stocks between 0 and 1.5 times the policy weighting, as described in chapter 3. For now assume that your policy is to be 100 percent invested in stocks so that the valuation model generates readings that range from 0 percent to 150 percent in stocks. Any time the price is above the moving average, I add 0.5 to the multiple, and any time the price is below the moving average, I take 0.5 off of the weighting. This generates a model that moves in 0.5 increments between –0.5 and 2.0 times the policy weighting.

The model accurately identifies six different market environments in which the average return on the S&P 500 has historically been higher at each and every incremental increase in exposure. Annually, this model has delivered 6.3 percent returns in excess of inflation. This means that if you began at age twenty-five and followed the model, you would have twice as much money after inflation by age fifty as you would if you simply bought the index and held it. By age seventy-four, you would have four times as much capital.

Combination Valuation and Technical
Model Back-Test Results

Stance	Weight	Count	Average	Std Dev	Sharpe Ratio	+95%	-95%
Very Bearish	-0.5	46	-1.53%	2.9%	-0.54	4.18%	-7.23%
Bearish	0.0	265	-1.52%	3.7%	-0.41	5.94%	-8.99%
Cautious	0.5	384	-0.44%	4.3%	-0.10	8.24%	-9.11%
Neutral	1.0	428	0.96%	3.6%	0.27	8.13%	-6.20%
Bullish	1.5	397	1.95%	3.4%	0.56	8.84%	-4.94%
Very Bullish	2.0	68	2.27%	6.9%	0.33	16.09%	-11.54%

Table 3: The S&P 500 model accurately identifies six different market
conditions, each with progressively more favorable risk-return characteristics.
By applying more weight to equities in the portfolio during periods
identified as more bullish and less weight in periods identified as bearish,
the model helps to both enhance long-term returns and reduce risks.

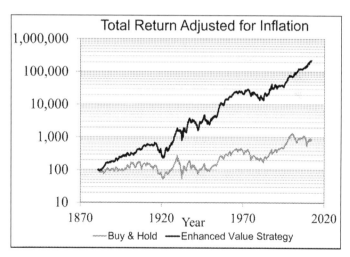

Chart 13: Trading on valuations alone beats the market, but adding
a timing element to the model improves performance dramatically.

Bonds

Most people buy bonds for the wrong reason. Most people think of bonds as a source of income, but considered purely as a source income, bonds are pretty pathetic. In almost every economic environment the United States has ever experienced, there have usually been better alternatives than bonds to secure high levels of income. Now that yields on most bonds are as low as or lower than at any other time in recorded history, the search for higher yields within the bond universe can drive investors to make extremely costly mistakes.

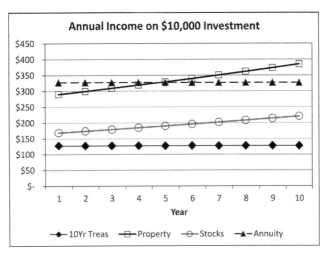

Chart 14: There are almost always better alternatives to bonds if one is interested purely in income.

The Right Reason to Buy Bonds

Stocks and real estate often generate higher levels of current income, have more favorable tax rates, and persistently deliver growth in income, which is something bonds can never do. Even fixed annuities, which are taxed the same as bonds and cannot grow, are nonetheless capable of generating much higher levels of fixed income than bonds.

The real reason to own bonds is their ability to go up when most other assets go down. In the last 140 years, there have only been two extended bear market periods when both bonds and equities lost purchasing power, and in both cases bonds nevertheless handily outperformed equities. The odds of losing purchasing power in any given ten-year period are about 30 percent for equity index investors and about 34 percent for bond index investors, but the odds of both asset classes losing purchasing power in any given ten-year period is only 21 percent.

It is this ability to go up when most other assets are going down that makes bonds attractive as an asset diversification tool, but clearly only some bonds have this ability. During the last real stress test of the markets, equities dropped 56.2 percent. At the same time, high-yield corporate bonds dropped 40.7 percent. High-quality corporate bonds dropped 24 percent. Preferred stocks dropped 56.4 percent. Real estate investment trusts dropped 66.1 percent High-dividend stocks dropped 67 percent. Emerging markets bonds dropped 33 percent. Long-term US treasuries rose 19 percent.

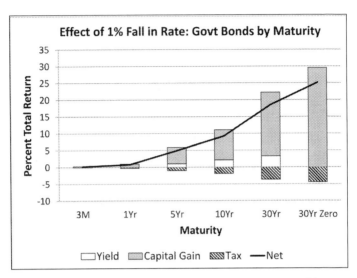

Chart 15: A 1 percent increase in interest rates could have a devastating effect on long-term bonds.

The lesson here is simple: buy bonds for protection, not for income. Bonds should be in your portfolio for one and only one reason, and this means that unlike equities, diversification is actually a very bad idea. There is only one kind of bond that serves this purpose adequately.

The United States is one of a handful of countries that have never failed to pay their obligations to creditors. No one who has ever bought a treasury note has yet received less than what was promised. Unless this changes, the value of bonds issued by the US Treasury will always increase when the value of other securities decline.

Never Chase Yield

The US government may of course one day join the thousands of other countries whose credit rating is less than perfect, but the amount of change in a bond's price will always be dependent on the quality of the issuer and the length of time to maturity. Longer-term bonds increase in price more than shorter-term bonds because there are more coupon payments that need to be adjusted to the new rate. A ten-year bond will have ten times as many payments as a one-year bond. So if interest rates change by 1 percent on a one-year bond, the bond price will usually change by about 1 percent, but a ten-year bond will change by about 9 percent. The reason the difference is not one for one is that the ten-year coupons occur in the future and must be discounted to compensate for the time value of money.

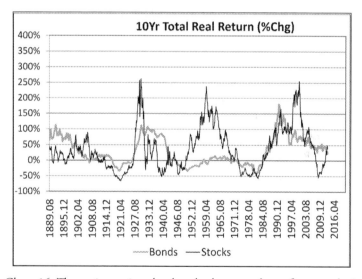

Chart 16: The entire notion that bonds always underperform stocks is derived from a single highly abnormal period between 1950 and 1970 when global inflation rose to rates unseen in more than one hundred years.

The quality of the issuer has a much larger impact. Historically, corporate bond issuers default on their obligations only about 1 percent of the time, so many investors are misled to believe the risk is very low for the amount of increased yield. Such investors are usually headed for an unpleasant surprise. The default rate on government bonds is a constant zero. The default on corporate bonds may average only 1 percent, but this rate is far from constant. During periods of economic stress, the rate can very easily rise to as much as 8 percent in any given year. Speculative grade bonds default about 2.6 percent of the time on average, but in any given year the rate has risen to as high as 15.4 percent. For these types of bonds then, when market participants fear a recession, rather than adjusting the interest rates downward and the bond prices upward, they adjust the interest rates upward and the bond prices downward. In other words, when you need them most, these bonds completely fail to serve any useful purpose. They are bonds in name only. In actual practice, they are not much different than equities.

For the yield on a one-year corporate bond to change from 6 percent to 9 percent, the price must fall 33 percent. For the yield to rise to 15 percent, the bond must fall 60 percent. The result is that the prices decline almost as much and sometimes even more horrendously than the price of high-quality stocks. To add insult to injury, the interest on speculative bonds is taxed as normal income, while the income and capital gains from stock investments are still taxed more favorably for most investors. About the only time speculative-grade bonds outperform high-quality bonds as an asset class is the same time stocks outperform bonds. If stocks are appropriately represented in your portfolio, there is no need to ever own any of these other hybrid instruments. They are redundant.

Beating the Bond Market

The bond market is even harder to predict than the stock market. The difference between holding short-term treasuries and long-term treasuries can be significant, but unlike stocks, there is no pattern of reverting to mean within the historical record. Bonds have moved in extremely long secular patterns, which by their nature are extremely difficult to predict. Anyone can see from hindsight that holding short-term bonds was better during the period from January 1954 to January 1981, but at all other times since 1934, it was better to hold long-term bonds. During this period, the real purchasing power of a long-term bond portfolio dropped 46 percent relative to the portfolio of short-term bonds. This is a big deal, and it offers a very neat opportunity in terms of efficiency because if you could effectively navigate these kinds of secular turning points, you only need to make one or two trades per lifetime and it would make enough difference to significantly change the way you live in retirement.

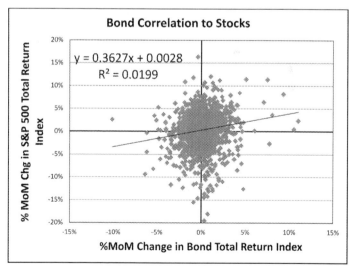

Chart 17: Monthly total returns on stocks and bonds have a very low level of correlation, making them excellent complements to each other in a diversified portfolio.

Unfortunately, if one is limited to information that would have been available in 1954, there is not much that would have enabled us to make an accurate forecast at the time the last downturn in bonds began. At the beginning of this period, inflation was a moderate 1.5 percent, the long bond yield was 2.8 percent, and the short bond yield was 1.4 percent. These are unremarkable numbers even now, and they were even less remarkable then. From that point, however, global inflation began to rise, slowly at first and then very rapidly, eventually peaking at around 12 percent. There was another period between 1907 and 1916 when the subsequent ten-year real returns on long-term bonds were negative, but I have been unable to find any reliable source of data on short-term rates during this period.

Chart 18: Long-term real returns on bonds were significantly negative in only three periods since 1879 and underperformed stocks only in the period between 1950 and 1970.

Consumer prices have risen at an average rate of 2.6 percent over the past 130 years, but in each period when long-term bonds lost purchasing power, the rate of inflation rose well above 4 percent. And while there is no shortage of people who think they can forecast inflation, there is a supreme lack of evidence that anyone really can. Economists used to believe that inflation was a function of unemployment, but it was precisely this period of bond underperformance that proved them wrong. This was the single worst period for bonds relative to equities ever in the recorded history of US financial markets, and it ended with very weak employment. Then economists began to believe that inflation was caused by excessive growth in the money supply. Milton Friedman, the leader of this revolt in economic theory, famously said, "Inflation is and everywhere has always been a monetary phenomenon" (Friedman 1963). This is still the prevailing wisdom today. It is extremely intuitive and alluring theory. If the quantity of money increases, the value of the money should decline relative to the fixed supply of goods. Unfortunately, this theory does not stand up to the test of actual historical data.

In his book *The Great Wave*, a study of 1500 years of inflation throughout the world, David Hackett Fisher demonstrates that many periods throughout recorded history have featured excessive money growth, yet inflation never ensued in the majority of these cases (Fisher 1996). The problem is that central bankers can print money, but they can't make bankers lend it out and they can't make people spend it. If the money sits in vaults and underneath mattresses, it never reaches circulation and cannot influence the level of general prices. We live in just such a time. Since the recession of 2008, the Fed has embarked on the most aggressive expansion of the money supply in history, yet we are experiencing one of the most stable pricing environments in all of recorded history. To the great consternation of followers of Milton Friedman's monetarist theory, no sign of inflation has yet to emerge.

Fisher alludes to the possibility that changes in the long-term rate of change in prices are more plausibly caused by shocks to the population, shocks such as war, plague, or discovery of gold in previously unpopulated areas. These are precisely the types of events that are simply unpredictable.

Today, we know from hindsight that the best time to maximize the long-bond portfolio was when interest rates hit 16 percent and the worst time, so far, was when they were only 2.8 percent back in the 1930s. But there is no real reason to believe there is anything special about either of these numbers. Peaks and troughs in yields have been far too rare to make any kind of statistically valid statement about them. Compared to the equity market, any forecasting model for the bond market is going to involve a greater deal of guesswork.

We can still take the same concept as the equity market and apply it broadly to the bond market. When yields are low, it should prove prudent to lower our exposure, and when they are high it should be better to increase our exposure. Even if the outlier period is removed, bond yields are still likely to peak and trough at different rates in each cycle. Just as with the equity market, a moving average can be used to determine the direction of the market. To make sure this directional indicator does not whipsaw into too many unprofitable trades, I can increase and decrease the sensitivity of the indicator in accordance with the level of yields.

The only problem is that unlike the equity markets, I just have to guess at what constitutes a high yield and what constitutes a low yield. Often in risk management, one is forced to make the best decision based on a list of unattractive choices.

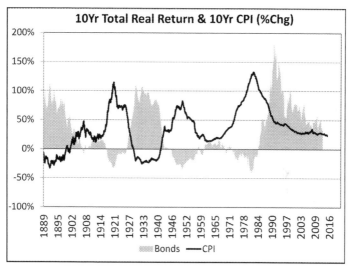

Chart 19: Accelerating rates of increases in bond
yields is always bad for bond investors.

If the model is based on data that is available going back to 1946
and the in-sample development period is cut off at May 1, 2003,
the low interest rate trigger will be 4.5 percent and the high interest
rate trigger will be 9.1 percent. Long-term bonds added 1.9 percent
in excess of inflation per year during the in-sample period and 2.1
percent during the out-of-sample period. The model returned 6.4
percent during the in-sample period and 1.9 percent during the
out-of-sample period.

For most people, bonds are never going to be the most important
driver of portfolio performance, but they are never going to be
an optional part either. If I can help you participate in the upside
potential of bonds while reducing even a modicum of the downside
risk, I've created an improvement of buy-and-hold that should be
important for all investors.

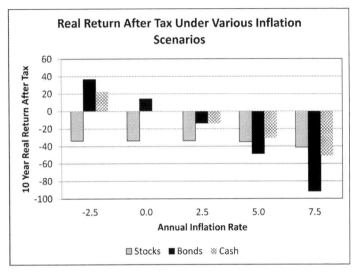

Chart 20: The bond-stock trade-off depends on
inflation, which is difficult to forecast.

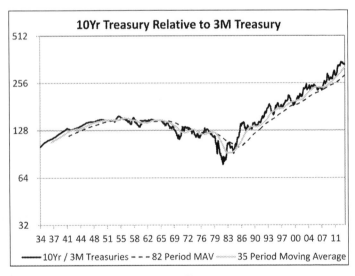

Chart 21: Performance of long-term treasuries is
marked by extremely long-term secular trends.

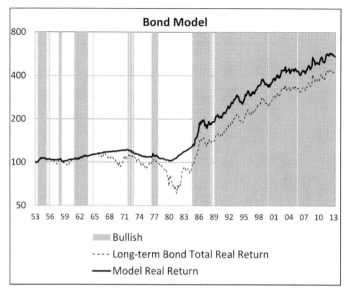

Chart 22: A multilayered trend analysis system helps capture the long-term secular bull market returns while curtailing exposure to the long-term secular bear markets.

CHAPTER 6

Gold

Why Inflation Damages the Stock-Bond Model

The stock-bond model described in previous chapters has suffered sustained declines in real purchasing power only twice in the past 140 years. The models I've presented in the previous two chapters suggest that at the time of this writing, the odds we are about to enter a third such period are abnormally high. If your only investments are in stocks and bonds, you might not be adequately diversified.

One of the greatest threats to the classic stock-bond strategy is the potential for unexpected fluctuations in inflation. Note that inflation itself is not a problem, because markets will price assets to compensate for any expected inflation. For example, inflation has averaged 2.1 percent in the United States for the last 140 years. The yield on ten-year bonds has averaged 4.7 percent, so there is a built-in premium above the expected rate of inflation.

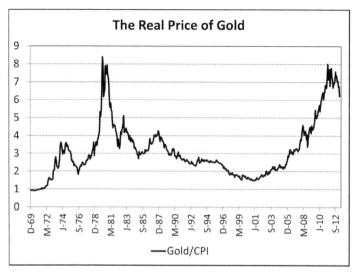

Chart 23: The real price of gold has experienced only one and a half complete cycles since it was allowed to float freely in 1970.

Unfortunately, inflation is one of the most poorly understood phenomena in all fields of economics, and expectations will almost always prove wrong during at least one very inconvenient stage in anyone's lifetime. Part of the reason for this lack of understanding is that bouts of extreme inflation are actually very rare in history. In *The Great Wave*, a book about the history of prices since the year 1264, David Hackett Fischer demonstrated that while prices have risen at an average rate of just 1 percent annually for the past eight hundred years, all of the inflation actually happened in four very finite periods, which he labeled great waves (Fischer 1996). Fischer named these periods the medieval, sixteenth-century, eighteenth-century, and twentieth-century price revolutions. Since these waves have happened only once every two hundred years, no human being has ever experienced more than one, and the vast majority of all human beings who have ever lived have never experienced even one of these waves of excessive inflation.

The reason these price revolutions are so different from normal times is not really the rate of inflation per se because if all prices were rising at the same rate, asset prices would easily compensate. The reason people experience pain during these periods is that prices of goods and services almost never rise uniformly. The cost of food, energy, and raw materials almost inevitably rise faster than wages and the cost of manufactured goods. This is why corporations who use raw materials to manufacture goods struggle to increase profits at the same pace as the rate of increase in general prices. Stock prices, reflecting the difficulty of such an environment, fail to keep pace, and bonds cannot perform the role of risk management because the rate of interest is fixed at levels that prevailed before the inflation started.

As rare as these price revolutions are, the consequences of being caught unprepared by one are too steep to ignore. There needs to be some form of protection in the portfolio that is entirely different from stocks or bonds.

Why Gold Solves the Problem (Even Though It Really Doesn't)

Warren Buffett recently stirred up a hornet's nest by pointing out that gold has no utility. Actually, he's been saying this at least since 1998 when he explained to an audience at the Harvard Club, "[Gold] gets dug out of the ground in Africa, or someplace. Then we melt it down, dig another hole, bury it again, and pay people to stand around guarding it. It has no utility. Anyone watching from Mars would be scratching their head" (Reeves 2012).

Between the time Buffett made this statement and late summer of 2012, gold rose some 470 percent, while stocks rose only 22 percent with dividends reinvested, proving that not even the smartest people in the world can always be right about their investments.

The ultimate utility of gold is its value as a diversification tool for investors in stocks and bonds. The scatter plots in charts 24 and 25 demonstrate this by plotting the price of gold against the other two assets. If gold prices were related to stocks or bonds, the dots on these two charts would line up in a pattern that fairly closely resembles a straight line. As you can see by the lack of any pattern whatsoever, there is virtually no relationship between gold and either of the other asset classes. This alone makes it an interesting and potentially useful diversification tool because any time the other two asset classes are losing value, gold is at least as likely to be gaining value as losing it.

Since gold was first allowed to float in 1971, it has undergone two magnificent bull markets, both of which coincided with equity bear markets and one that coincided with the worst bond bear market in US history. The first gold bull market began immediately after gold prices were first allowed to float in 1971 and culminated in an 800 percent rise in real terms by the end of 1979. The second bull market began in 2001 and as of this writing looks as if it ended in 2012 with another 530 percent rise in real terms.

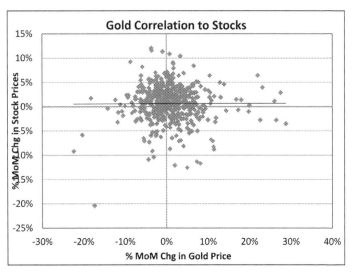

Chart 24: Real gold returns have effectively
zero correlation to real stock returns.

Needless to say, however, gold is more useful as a hedge when it is both uncorrelated and also rising in real terms. Investors found cold comfort from gold's noncorrelation between 1978 and 2000 when the metal lost 82 percent of its real purchasing power. The ability of gold to generate these kinds of losses for this length of time makes it impossible to hold the metal as a long-term core investment. In fact, most retirement plans do not allow you to invest in gold for this reason. Retirement plan sponsors do not want to risk getting sued, so they don't even offer you the choice of investing in gold. The real problem with gold is that there is no way to appraise its true value. Warren Buffett was right about this: gold doesn't have a yield, so there is no way to calculate the net present value of future cash flows.

Numerous forecasters have tried a number of macroeconomic factors such as inflation, exchange rates, real interest rates, measures of financial system stability, growth in the balance sheets of central banks, and many others. Most of these methods do a very poor job of explaining past moves in the price of gold, and all of them suffer from at least one fatal flaw. If you are going to make a ten-year investment in gold on the basis of a complex combination of these factors, then you have to accurately forecast all of the factors in this combination for the next ten years. Let's be realistic. No one has actually ever been able to make such accurate long-term forecasts of any one of these factors, let alone all of them at once.

Just the same, it helps to understand what these factors are and why some people believe they are influential.

Inflation

The presumed correlation to inflation is the most popular reason to buy gold, yet it is the least substantiated. Just look at chart 25 showing the relationship of changes in the price of gold to the changes in consumer prices. The correlation is effectively zero. Gold advocates have come up with a large number of ridiculous explanations for this. The most common is that even though gold is not correlated to inflation in the short-term, gold tends to hold its value over long periods of time. If you are a risk manager trying to explain that one to your boss in a multibillion-dollar hedge fund, good luck keeping your job. If you need to hedge inflation, say in 2008, it isn't going to help you if gold holds its value in 2012. If something is sometimes correlated and sometimes not, mathematicians would say that it is simply *not* correlated.

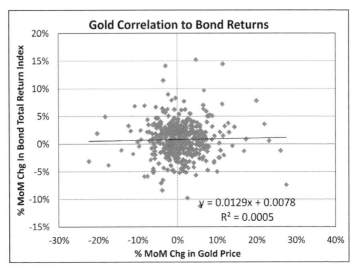

Chart 25: Real gold returns have effectively
zero correlation to real bond returns.

More importantly, there's nothing special about an asset holding
its value against inflation. Anything that isn't perishable will increase
in value against the dollar over time if the value of the dollar declines,
which is what happens when there is inflation. A good investment
should not just hold its value. It should increase in value. At any rate,
gold has achieved some of its greatest returns of all time in the past
several years, at a time when both the actual inflation rate and the
expected inflation rate have moderated. This doesn't make any sense
if gold is merely an inflation hedge.

The US Exchange Rate

The exchange rate factor acts similarly to inflation except that there
have been a few occasions in history when the value of the dollar
has depreciated against a basket of other currencies without resulting
in any subsequent bouts of inflation. In such cases, gold has always

performed well against the dollar, but so have stocks and other currencies. US companies, especially large-cap stocks in the S&P 500, earn a substantial share of their profits from overseas operations, and any time the dollar weakens, not only do US companies become more competitive, but the earnings they generate overseas become more valuable in dollar terms. So although gold does well in these periods, you don't really need it for this purpose because stocks should do just fine.

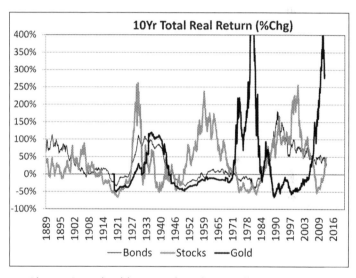

Chart 26: Real gold returns have been stellar exactly when stock and bond investors needed them to be stellar.

Real Interest Rates

In my view, this is the biggest problem for gold. It costs money to store gold, so there is a real opportunity cost to holding it, and on a couple of occasions, significant changes in real interest rates have coincided with very significant changes in the real price of gold. This appears to be the most plausible explanation for the doubling of the real price of gold in the four years from 2008 to 2012, when there was no discernible change in inflation or inflation expectations priced into any other asset markets, but the real interest rate on ten-year treasuries dropped from nearly 6 percent to –2 percent. Our concern here is that the correlation between gold and bonds increased; if this represents a permanent change in the behavior of gold investments relative to bonds, then it is no longer reasonable to expect gold to protect us against declines in our bonds.

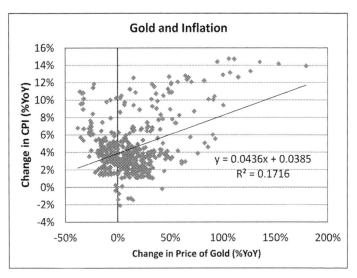

Chart 27: Contrary to popular belief, gold returns are not correlated to inflation either.

Credit Default Premium

The spread between AAA and BBB bonds has had a significant correlation between the real price of gold, but during the two most important episodes of default risk contagion, during the 2000–2002 and 2007–2008 bear markets, the protection provided by gold was weak. Bonds did a much better job in these two episodes. Whenever credit contagion is a global phenomenon, the dollar has been strong, which has weakened the price of gold while strengthening the price of bonds. Even when gold has seemed to be somewhat correlated to the default spread, the fact that gold consistently lead the default spread suggests it is not the default spread that predicts gold but rather gold that predicts the default spread.

Fed Balance Sheet

Milton Friedman is solely responsible for one of the most common myths in the marketplace today. His original explanation of inflation, namely that it is "always and everywhere a monetary phenomenon in the sense that it is and can be produced only by a more rapid increase in the quantity of money than in output" (Friedman 1963) is so simple and self-evident that no one ever questions it, but unfortunately it is a very misleading statement. During the 1820s and 1830s, the money supply trebled in fifteen years, but the CPI rose less than 1 percent annually throughout the period. Similarly, large swings in the money supply in the 1840s and 1850s caused almost no change in general price levels. Similar examples have been recorded throughout the world in the record of historical prices of the past eight hundred years. Unless the newly produced money finds its way into circulation, it does not and cannot influence prices. In the past four years, the Fed balance sheet has expanded 1373 percent, but there has been no meaningful change in the rate of inflation. Contrary to what the monetarists refuse to believe, this disconnect between money growth and inflation is not at all abnormal.

Gold bulls love to borrow the techniques of apocalyptic cults. Every time the predicted day of reckoning fails to materialize, they reschedule it. The argument goes something like, "If an x-fold expansion of the money base hasn't caused inflation by now, then surely some of that money will eventually find its way into the market and inflation will only be delayed." History has shown that there is no certainty in this statement at all.

The Fed's balance sheet appears to have had some correlation with the real price of gold between 1978 and 2004, but it is easier to ascribe this correlation to pure chance than to find a causal rationale for this behavior, and at any rate, the model falters badly thereafter. If this were the only factor affecting the real price of gold, then gold would today be eight times its current price. I am entirely uncomfortable with models that fail by this magnitude for even a short period of time, let alone four years running.

Beating the Gold Market

So far I have been talking about ways people have tried to explain the price of gold, and I hope it has become clear that no one really knows what drives the price of gold. Even if someone did, forecasting the price of gold more than ten years forward would require a forecast of all of the explanatory variables ten years into the future, which is simply not plausible. No one has ever made this many long-term forecasts with enough accuracy to be even remotely useful.

There is an argument to be made that you should just own gold as an insurance policy. You don't expect to make money off your home insurance, but you still wouldn't consider owning a home without insuring it. Advisors who make this argument typically suggest putting 5 to 10 percent of your assets in gold. If you lose 80 percent of 5 percent, it's only a 4 percent loss. These advisors would argue that 4 percent is not such a terrible price to pay for insurance, but I would beg to differ. First of all, placing 5 percent of your assets in gold will never come close to providing adequate insurance for your entire portfolio. The only period that our stock-bond model lost significant value and there was an open market for gold was between February 1973 and July 1982. During this period, the stock bond model lost 55 percent of its purchasing power while gold gained 122 percent. To insure a $100,000 portfolio of stocks and bonds, one would have needed $45,000 worth of gold. Imagine paying $45,000 on insurance for a $100,000 home!

Another reason gold is a lousy insurance vehicle is that you can get better coverage in the option market for much less than 1 percent.

If there were a way to put gold on an even footing with stocks and bonds and purchase it as an investment rather than just an insurance policy, it would make sense to place a larger portion of one's assets in gold. The tentatively good news is that there probably is.

To do so we have to recognize a very different set of rules and objectives than we did with the stock and bond models. With those models, we were looking to buy assets below their intrinsic value and sell above intrinsic value while minimizing the volatility of returns. With gold, we have no idea what intrinsic value is or even what it could be, but we want to be certain we are fully invested during the massive speculative rallies that have driven the price up hundreds of percentage points within a period of a few years. As a secondary objective, we want to minimize the cost of holding gold during its periodic but devastatingly long periods of decline.

It turns out that for technical analysts, who look only at price action and do not care about value, this is not such a difficult objective to meet. The only problem with technical analysis is it tends to be very short-term; thus, returns are subject to much higher tax rates. To minimize this problem, I've used a multiple moving average technique that is very effective at reducing the amount of trades. Basically, to invest in gold, I require the current price of gold to be above the four-week moving average; the four-week moving average to be above the thirteen-week moving average; and the thirteen-week moving average to be above the fourteen-week moving average.

To exit the trade, I use a slightly more sensitive combination of two, thirteen, and seventeen. When the signal is positive, I buy GLD—an ETF that invests 100 percent of its assets in gold bullion and has very low operating costs. Unlike a large number of commodity funds that only invest in futures, GLD very reliably tracks the price of actual gold. Whenever the signal is negative, I transfer the funds to BND, the Vanguard Total Bond Index Fund.

The total return for actual gold bullion over the entire forty-four-year period in which gold prices were allowed to fluctuate has been 3,482 percent, or 8.5 percent per year. During the same period, the return on ten-year treasuries was 2,611 percent, or 7.8 percent annually. My model, however, was up 15,871 percent, or 12.2 percent annually, with far less volatility. With gold, 95 percent of weekly returns are between 2.9 percent and –2.55 percent. With my model, 95 percent of weekly returns are between 2.53 percent and –2.03 percent.

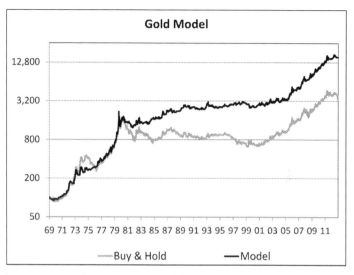

Chart 28: Very slow-moving trend-following indicators capture most of the bull markets in gold while avoiding most of the bear markets.

The only problem with the gold model is that it is based on a much less historical precedent than either the stock or bond models. Despite nearly forty years of trading freely on open markets, gold's total return has basically come in two massive vertical leaps interspersed by one very long bear market. It is as if one had three months of data for the stock market, two up and one down, and on the basis of that, one projected 0.6 percent monthly returns. Alas, nothing is ever certain in investments, and a person often has to act on the basis of what is known, because by the time something becomes certain, he or she might literally be dead.

Ultimately, investing in gold requires just that kind of judgment call. To make such a call, it is helpful to think about what might go wrong. In my view, the biggest risk would be that gold stops moving in secular trends and falls prey to much choppier price movements. If that were to happen, the moving average signal the model is based on would react too slowly, and profits would dwindle or possibly even disappear. In such a scenario, the potential losses would still be fairly minor, since by its very nature, a choppier price pattern would entail less extreme price movements. In my judgment, the potential benefits of using this model far outweigh the potential risks for most investors.

CHAPTER 7

Cash

During every crisis, someone will bring up the idea that cash is king, but it's really never more than the court jester. The income from cash accounts is taxed at normal income rates, which for most investors are higher than the capital gains tax rate, and the pretax rate rarely compensates you for inflation. Between 1934 and 2013, the average after-tax inflation-adjusted return on three-month government bills was –0.9 percent per year. As seen in previous chapters, though, the expected returns on other assets can be as bad as –1.5 percent per month when the models turn negative. The fact is that cash outperformed all other asset classes in 13.8 percent of the months since 1969. You should never be afraid to hold cash for defensive purposes during short periods of time.

Conventional wisdom typically calls for you to build a reserve fund of between three and six months' cash requirements, depending on your job security, but if you have good credit, today it is possible to use a line of credit for emergency purposes, provided you don't actually spend the line of credit on a new patio. In reality, holding any more cash than absolutely necessary is almost always a bad strategic move, so if you have a line of credit for emergency purposes, there is no reason to hold more than a month's worth of your essential expenditures in cash. For almost any investor under fifty, cash is going to be held for such short periods of time that you really don't need to pay any attention to it.

Once you pass the age of fifty, however, the importance of wealth preservation starts to increase rapidly. At this age, as mentioned in chapter 3, the net present value of your future savings starts to decrease very rapidly, and hopefully you are replacing it with rapidly growing investment assets at this point. But once investments become a substantial part of your net worth, protecting that net worth becomes increasingly difficult, and suddenly, cash takes on more significant strategic importance. The system described in this book has extremely low volatility compared to the returns it is capable of generating, but there is simply no way to guarantee these returns. There is always risk in stocks, bonds, and gold, no matter how well you mix them or how well you can time them.

Cash Alternatives

If you cannot tolerate a drawdown of 15 percent in a single year, the only way to avoid that risk with certainty is to increase the policy allocation to cash or other forms of guaranteed return products. When cash becomes a long-term proposition, there are several other more interesting options that serve the same purpose of reducing volatility but offer less liquidity. These include bank certificates of deposit, structured products, annuities, and some forms of cash-value life insurance.

The first avenue most older investors lean toward is the one that is easiest to understand and most familiar, but it is probably the least attractive. This is the certificate of deposit, which—by sacrificing liquidity—gives you the right to a very slightly higher yield that is nonetheless guaranteed.

If you are willing to forgo the liquidity feature, certificates of deposit can be purchased with maturities ranging anywhere from three months to five years. You can spend the money earlier, but you will forfeit the interest and usually pay a penalty. At the time of this writing, one bank was offering three-month CDs at an annual percentage yield of 0.07 percent—effectively nothing. The same bank offered twelve-month CDs at 0.31 percent, two-year CDs at 0.63 percent, three-year CDs at 1.15 percent, four-year CDs at 1.5 percent, and five-year at 2.0 percent.

Yields might vary somewhat from one bank to another, but you can get the idea from this example that the longer you lock up your money, the higher the rate you will receive. The risk you take with such instruments is that while your money is locked up, market rates might rise and you will not be in a position to take advantage of the higher yield. This is why most advisors suggest you layer your money across several maturities so you always have at least one CD maturing per year that will give you the opportunity to rollover into a higher-yielding instrument.

Unfortunately, bank CDs almost never offer attractive yields at any maturity relative to other instruments that are just as safe or in some cases even safer.

At the time of this writing, money market accounts with $100,000 or higher were yielding 0.65 percent. These accounts are liquid. You can write checks against them and spend the money any way you like at any time. Some even offer an ATM card. Money market rates will automatically rise whenever the interest on short-term instruments rise, so there is no risk of missing out on higher rates. Already, there is no reason to own a bank CD of any maturity less than two years because these sacrifice both liquidity *and* yield!

Guaranteed Income for Life

A far better alternative in almost every circumstance is provided by annuities. There are thousands of different kinds of annuities, but the only ones you really need to understand for this purpose are simple fixed annuities.

Let's start with an example of a fifty-year-old woman who wants to invest $100,000 in a guaranteed-income product. She does not need the money anytime soon, so she purchases a fixed annuity with payouts deferred until she is sixty-five, which is when she expects to retire. At current rates published by one insurance company, the annual payments at age sixty-five will be $11,500. These payments are guaranteed for as long as she lives. If she puts the same amount of money in a money market fund, assuming interest rates do not ever change, and after allowing the money to accumulate for ten years, she begins to withdraw $11,500 per year, her money will be gone by the age of seventy-four. If she puts the money in a ten-year bond fund, even at the current rate of 2.6 percent, her money will be gone before she is seventy-five.

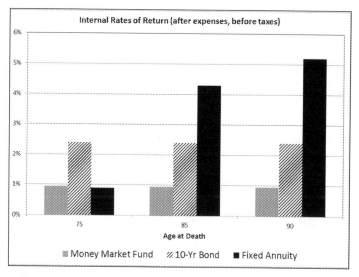

Chart 29: Assuming that market rates remain unchanged, only annuity contracts can guarantee that the internal rate of return will rise for investors who live long enough. Rates on money market and bond market funds are subject to change.

One could also argue that the annuity payments are safer than the bank payments. Banks take your money and loan it back out to entities of which you have no knowledge and over which you have no control. They are allowed to lend nine times as much as their equity, and frequently enough they make mistakes that cause them to go into liquidation. People who make deposits of up to $100,000 are guaranteed by the federal government to get their money back, but for any amount over this number, you are on your own. Insurance companies, on the other hand, are only allowed to lend as much money as they have, and no insurance company in the United States has ever failed to pay a claim because of lack of funds. If you buy an annuity for any amount of dollars from any insurance company with a favorable rating from any of the independent rating agencies, there is really no plausible scenario in which you would not get paid.

What to Watch Out For

If you've been reading carefully, there should be a question burning in your head: If insurance companies are safer than banks, why should they be able to pay a rate of 11.5 percent when banks are paying less than 1 percent?

There are two reasons. The first is that the insurance company is not paying you an interest rate of 11.5 percent. A very large part of the payment you receive is your own money just being returned to you. You could do this yourself by putting your money in a money market fund and making a payment to yourself of $11,500 per year, but your money would not last as long. The reason insurance companies can make the payments last longer is that only an insurance company is able to pool the assets of multiple investors together and thereby use the funds from those who die at younger ages to pay those who live longer.

When a fifty-year-old woman of average health purchases an annuity, the insurance company calculates that she will live to the age of eighty-six. Since payments are delayed until age sixty-five, the insurance company calculates that there will be twenty-one payments. Since the money is allowed to accumulate for ten years before the first payment is made, the insurance company calculates how much the money is likely to grow in those years. Let's say that at 5 percent, the money is expected to reach $160,000. The insurance company then divides this into twenty-one payments of approximately $7,700. Of this, $4,762 will constitute a return of principal. Another $2,038 represents return of the interest earned during the deferral period. The remaining $3,800 is current interest on the new principal of $160,000. This amounts to about a 2.3 percent interest rate.

The second reason insurance companies are able to pay a higher rate than banks is that within the pool of annuity owners, some will die before the expected time and some will live much longer. The insurance company uses the funds from those who die young to pay those who live beyond the normal expectancy. The actual rate of return you receive depends on how long you live. In this way, annuities are the opposite of life insurance. The longer you live, the higher the rate of return. In the case above, if the woman lives to age eighty-four as expected, the internal rate of return on this annuity is 4.3 percent. If she lives to age ninety-four, the rate of return increases to 5.3 percent. But if she dies at age seventy-two, the rate of return is only 0.9 percent.

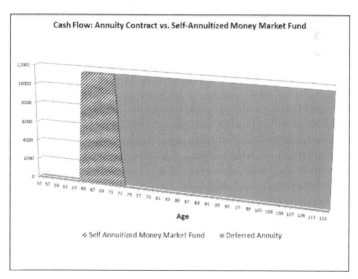

Chart 30: Any investor can self-annuitize a money market fund, but the money will run out quickly. Only a life insurance company can enter contracts that guarantee a fixed income for as long as you live.

Since the average long-term rate of return on equities has been 3.5 percent plus inflation over the ages and inflation has averaged 2 percent, even the most volatile and aggressive investment stance might earn you only 5.5 percent per year over a thirty-year period. When you think about this, locking in a 4.3 percent rate that is guaranteed every year for as long as you live can have a tremendous impact on stabilizing and even increasing your total return.

The income from annuities is taxed the same way as cash and other short-term instruments, but annuities are still used as effective tax-management tools because of the ability to defer income and because principal is not taxed. In the case above, there is no tax until payments begin. Once payments begin, the portion that represents the return of principal is not taxed, but the remaining amount is taxed at the rate of your personal income taxes. Once this principal is exhausted, you will be charged a tax on the entire amount of any further payments.

The main thing to remember about an annuity is that it is a contract between an insurance company and an individual. As such, it is highly individualized compared to a bond, equity, or commodity, so I cannot go into all the necessary details in a book like this. Neither can I document historical returns in any model. You should consult your accountant or advisor about how annuities can fit into your particular situation. Suffice it to say that whenever taking risk is not an option, there might be an annuity product that can generate higher and possibly even safer returns than cash.

CHAPTER 8

Real Estate

Many people feel more comfortable with real estate than they do with stocks or bonds. Once you move out of your parents' home, you either rent or buy, and from that point on, you are closer and more familiar to the idea of running a real estate business than most people ever become with running any other kind of business. This is not a bad idea for individuals willing to spend the time and energy to actually run a small business, but you should understand that real estate is not a passive investment. You must get involved in the actual running of it. There are plenty of other books to help you learn how to do this. My only intention is to help you decide whether or not to do it.

The biggest mistake anyone can make is to think his or her home is an investment. You should be very clear on one thing: your first home is an expense. You only become a real estate investor when you've purchased your second home and have rented it out to someone you've never met before.

Your Home Is *Not* an Investment

According to the Case-Shiller Index of home prices, home prices rose at a compound average rate of 3.8 percent annually from 1987 to 2012. This data set only gives us three recessions to look at, but it is widely considered to be the best data available on housing. At least it includes periods of both rising and falling interest rates. The 3.8 percent annual rise compares to the average CPI of 2.9 percent during the same period. In comparison, the S&P 500 returned 7.3 percent during the same period.

Unfortunately, this comparison greatly overstates the actual return of owning a home. Unlike stocks, you have to pay a 6 percent commission to a broker when you buy a home, and you have considerable expenses while you own it. You have to fix a leaking roof, and you have to pay property taxes. If I very conservatively estimate these expenses at 1 percent annually, your return falls to 2.8 percent, essentially just keeping up with inflation. It is probably more realistic to assume costs will be higher than this, especially with older houses. If you need to withdraw cash from your savings for any unexpected expense, you can usually sell bonds or stocks at the most recent market price within seconds. Selling a house may take months, and you are very unlikely to get the price you want at the time you want to sell.

One objection to this analysis that could be raised is that most people don't pay cash for their homes. Many real estate investment experts claim that the most attractive feature of owning your own home is the ability to borrow at favorable rates. These so-called experts are making another false assumption that will cost you money if you believe them. Borrowing money is only an advantage if the interest rate you pay is lower than the returns you gain on your capital. Most of the time, this isn't the case. The average rate on a thirty-year mortgage during the period was 7.1 percent, so over the entire period, the average cost of borrowing exceeded the rate of return on the asset. Of course, the actual return you experience will depend on your credit rating, your income tax rate, and the timing of your purchase, but gearing up on your home generally will not make it a better investment.

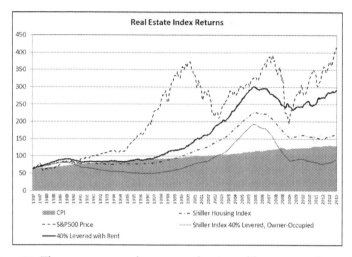

Chart 31: The returns on real estate are dominated by rent, not by capital appreciation. If you don't rent the building, it is not an investment.

This doesn't mean you shouldn't buy a house, but you should first rid yourself of the delusion that you are guaranteed to come out ahead for no other reason than the passage of time. The decision to buy a home should be based entirely on where you want to live and what it costs to buy relative to the cost of renting at the time of your decision. The *New York Times* has a decent tool for calculating the difference between renting and buying for your individual situation. You can find this tool on the Internet at the following URL: http://www.nytimes.com/interactive/business/buy-rent-calculator. html?ref=realestate&_r=0.

This tool gives you the ability to input the home price, the rent, the down payment, the mortgage rate, and the annual property taxes. It will then calculate the relative gain or loss from buying in each year of ownership. I plugged in the current nationwide median home price of $221,000, the average rental rate of 4.9 percent (which works out to $898 per month), and the current rate on a thirty-year fixed mortgage of 4.35 percent. I assumed annual property taxes of 1.35 percent not only because that is the default suggested by the *New York Times* but also because it squares with my own experience of owning properties in three different states. When I assumed a down payment of 20 percent, the *New York Times* tool told me that if I was planning to stay for any period less than fourteen years, I was better off renting. If I purchased the home and owned it for fourteen years, I would save $39 a year over the cost of renting. If I owned it for thirty years, I would save $3,821 a year.

The *New York Times* model is fairly sophisticated in that it takes into account commissions on purchase, repair and maintenance charges, and numerous tax consequences. But what it does not take into account is what you could have done with that down payment if you had not purchased a home. If you had invested that $44,000 in the asset allocation model described in this book, you might have made an average 11 percent, or $4,880 per year, from year one. If you continued to rent while investing no more than the initial principal into this strategy, by year fourteen, you would have averaged $10,400 per year from your investment. By year thirty, the average annual return rises to $32,100. From a purely economic standpoint, there is never a reason to own a home. If the game is to die with the most amount of money, renters always win.

This, of course, is not the goal of the game of life. There are other reasons to own a home other than investment purposes. You might want to have pets, you might want to live in a certain location, or maybe you would like to raise chickens in your backyard. There are a lot of really nice things you can do with your own home that you cannot do while you live in someone else's. But it is extremely important not to confuse your home with an investment. A home will never serve that purpose well.

This conclusion should affect the way you decide on a location. If you think of your home as an investment, you are likely to buy as much home as you can afford. Indeed, this is what most experts advised, at least until 2008. But if it is just a place to live and a way to save money over renting, then you should buy the smallest home you think you can feel comfortable in. Take the money you save and invest it in something that really makes sense as a long-term investment.

Owning a Second Home

None of this conversation should be taken to mean that nonowner occupied real estate is a bad investment. Rental rates are almost always higher than yield on bonds and are also almost always higher than the cost of a mortgage. You can write off both depreciation and interest expenses and even repair charges against your income taxes. And finally, the revenue typically grows a little faster than the costs. When normal rental income, less a management fee of 10 percent, is added to the Shiller index, assuming moderate leverage of 20 percent, the expected rate of return comes to about 7.2 percent annually. This is nearly identical to the return achieved by the S&P 500 including dividends, and it was achieved with considerably less volatility. This rate of return assumes zero vacancy rates, which is unrealistic in any market. A more realistic expectation based on the unit being vacant on average one month per year would give you a return of 6.6 percent. This is still not bad, and current mortgage rates are below historical averages while rental rates are still quite attractive at the time of this writing.

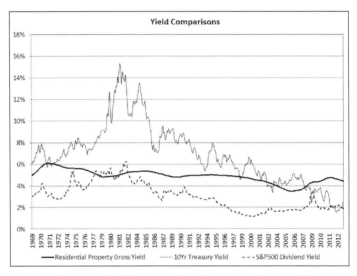

Chart 32: Yields on residential property have held
up better than most other asset classes.

In an ideal world, real estate should return more than stocks and
bonds because it is far less liquid. You can purchase shares in the
S&P 500 for as little as $1,000, and you can liquidate whenever you
want. You can sell it and then change your mind and buy it back in
the same day. Real estate can take many months to purchase and
even as long as a year or more to sell. A typical real estate investment
normally requires the establishment of credit and a minimum down
payment of $20,000 to $30,000. In our example, it requires $45,000.
In my opinion, you should at least get compensated for the lack of
liquidity.

If you've been paying attention throughout this book, there's a
burning question in your mind right now: How likely is it that an
individual investor actually makes the index returns? As you should
know by now, it is pretty unlikely.

Neighborhoods decline. Some houses, for no discernible rhyme or reason, need more repairs than others. Tax rates change. Vacancies are irregular and unpredictable. Natural disasters can wipe out everything, and even with insurance you usually can't recover the lost rental income. Returns differ by region and location as well. In Portland, home prices rose at a compound annual rate of 5 percent between 1987 and 2012, while in Las Vegas the rate was only 1.7 percent. Since it takes a minimum of five to six years before a typical property can be profitable, even if it is always rented out, the question is if you can forecast which houses in which areas will perform the best over the next six to ten years.

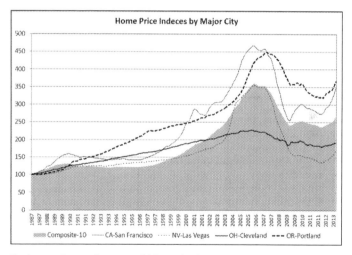

Chart 33: Even if you could buy the best investment home in any given city, there is virtually no possibility that you could predict which city would generate the best returns for your real estate business.

Most people can't buy twenty homes in a variety of states and neighborhoods. Unless you are extremely wealthy, a properly diversified portfolio of homes is out of the question. This brings up the final topic of this discussion, which is the real estate investment trust and its various derivations. With this kind of instrument, you solve the diversification problem and meet the passive investment requirement, but you create a new problem that no one in the real estate business tells you about. Namely, if you buy a listed fund, you are no longer buying a separate asset class; you're buying a stock, plain and simple.

The greatest source of change in stock prices is the change in the multiple on earnings, not the change in earnings. The multiple of any listed real estate company is likely to be affected by the same things that affect the multiple on earnings of any other business. In fact, when US stocks dropped 41 percent in 2008, the real estate index dropped 61 percent. An asset class with that kind of risk-return profile simply doesn't serve any useful purpose. That's the main reason I didn't include real estate anywhere in the asset allocation model described in this book.

For some individuals in certain circumstances, unlisted real estate funds might make some sense if you could find a reputable manager. You're buying a direct participation in a company that operates real estate properties and is not subject to stock market fluctuations. It is noncorrelated, it is a passive investment, and it is typically well diversified. It is still absolutely essential that you confirm that the fund you own is managed conservatively and that it actually owns more than twenty properties. I have seen too many of these funds go to zero because they concentrated all their assets in one or two properties that ended up shutting down and selling out at less than the value of outstanding liabilities. Be careful to inspect detailed performance records of the manager and make sure that they very specifically spell out their current yields. All too often, even if the REIT is well diversified, the yield, after all expenses, is no better than safer and more liquid assets. Unfortunately, the financial advisor from whom you would typically buy such funds is often paid a very high sales commission, making it unlikely that you will get very honest advice. Typically, there is no secondary market for these instruments, so they are even less liquid than an individual home. Assume that once you buy such an asset, you will never be able to sell it. Good investments can be found in this space, but it is not easy. Be very careful, and if there is any doubt, go without.

CHAPTER 9

A Final Warning

I hope you have enjoyed our journey, and if you have learned anything, I hope it is that you should always question conventional wisdom, which is almost always wrong. My final warning, however, is that financial markets are always evolving, and there will always be some new product or fad that will seem to command your attention. Somewhere in the world, there will always be someone who has made a fortune in some new craze that will fall outside the range of subjects covered in this book and allow its followers to proclaim, "This time it is different."

For many more poor fools who find out too late, the temptation to get involved in something they have very little understanding of will be too overwhelming. They will buy at the top, and they will be wiped out again. Somewhere in the world, this is probably already happening.

Whether or not you find the solution I've provided useful or not, at least for the vast majority of individual investors, investment income over an entire career will never come close to matching the amount of income you can earn from concentrating on your career and just making certain that you save at least 10 percent of your income every year.

If you wish to execute the strategy I've outlined in this book on your own and would like to receive a spreadsheet with the necessary data and links to sites where you can get regular updates, please send an e-mail to mallen@astonresearch.com with the words "request spreadsheet" in the subject line.

APPENDIX: AGE-BASED POLICY AND TACTICS ALLOCATION TABLES

| Asset Allocation Formula for a 20-Year Old | | | | | | | | | | |
| Policy | | | Tactical Models | | | Actual Weight | | | | |
SPY	TLT	GLD	SPY	TLT	GLD	SPY	TLT	GLD	BND	MMkt
80%	10%	10%	-50%	100%	100%	-40%	10%	10%	80%	40%
80%	10%	10%	-50%	0%	100%	-40%	0%	10%	0%	130%
80%	10%	10%	-50%	100%	0%	-40%	10%	0%	80%	50%
80%	10%	10%	-50%	0%	0%	-40%	0%	0%	0%	140%
80%	10%	10%	0%	100%	100%	0%	10%	10%	80%	0%
80%	10%	10%	0%	0%	100%	0%	0%	10%	0%	90%
80%	10%	10%	0%	100%	0%	0%	10%	0%	80%	10%
80%	10%	10%	0%	0%	0%	0%	0%	0%	0%	100%
80%	10%	10%	50%	100%	100%	40%	10%	10%	40%	0%
80%	10%	10%	50%	0%	100%	40%	0%	10%	0%	50%
80%	10%	10%	50%	100%	0%	40%	10%	0%	50%	0%
80%	10%	10%	50%	0%	0%	40%	0%	0%	0%	60%
80%	10%	10%	100%	100%	100%	80%	10%	10%	0%	0%
80%	10%	10%	100%	0%	100%	80%	0%	10%	0%	10%
80%	10%	10%	100%	100%	0%	80%	10%	0%	10%	0%
80%	10%	10%	100%	0%	0%	80%	0%	0%	0%	20%
80%	10%	10%	150%	100%	100%	120%	10%	10%	0%	-40%
80%	10%	10%	150%	0%	100%	120%	0%	10%	0%	-30%
80%	10%	10%	150%	100%	0%	120%	10%	0%	0%	-30%
80%	10%	10%	150%	0%	0%	120%	0%	0%	0%	-20%
80%	10%	10%	200%	100%	100%	160%	10%	10%	0%	-80%
80%	10%	10%	200%	0%	100%	160%	0%	10%	0%	-70%
80%	10%	10%	200%	100%	0%	160%	10%	0%	0%	-70%
80%	10%	10%	200%	0%	0%	160%	0%	0%	0%	-60%

Table 4

Asset Allocation Formula for a 30-Year Old										
Policy			Tactical Models			Actual Weight				
SPY	TLT	GLD	SPY	TLT	GLD	SPY	TLT	GLD	BND	MMkt
70%	15%	15%	-50%	100%	100%	-35%	15%	15%	70%	35%
70%	15%	15%	-50%	0%	100%	-35%	0%	15%	0%	120%
70%	15%	15%	-50%	100%	0%	-35%	15%	0%	70%	50%
70%	15%	15%	-50%	0%	0%	-35%	0%	0%	0%	135%
70%	15%	15%	0%	100%	100%	0%	15%	15%	70%	0%
70%	15%	15%	0%	0%	100%	0%	0%	15%	0%	85%
70%	15%	15%	0%	100%	0%	0%	15%	0%	70%	15%
70%	15%	15%	0%	0%	0%	0%	0%	0%	0%	100%
70%	15%	15%	50%	100%	100%	35%	15%	15%	35%	0%
70%	15%	15%	50%	0%	100%	35%	0%	15%	0%	50%
70%	15%	15%	50%	100%	0%	35%	15%	0%	50%	0%
70%	15%	15%	50%	0%	0%	35%	0%	0%	0%	65%
70%	15%	15%	100%	100%	100%	70%	15%	15%	0%	0%
70%	15%	15%	100%	0%	100%	70%	0%	15%	0%	15%
70%	15%	15%	100%	100%	0%	70%	15%	0%	15%	0%
70%	15%	15%	100%	0%	0%	70%	0%	0%	0%	30%
70%	15%	15%	150%	100%	100%	105%	15%	15%	0%	-35%
70%	15%	15%	150%	0%	100%	105%	0%	15%	0%	-20%
70%	15%	15%	150%	100%	0%	105%	15%	0%	0%	-20%
70%	15%	15%	150%	0%	0%	105%	0%	0%	0%	-5%
70%	15%	15%	200%	100%	100%	140%	15%	15%	0%	-70%
70%	15%	15%	200%	0%	100%	140%	0%	15%	0%	-55%
70%	15%	15%	200%	100%	0%	140%	15%	0%	0%	-55%
70%	15%	15%	200%	0%	0%	140%	0%	0%	0%	-40%

Table 5

Asset Allocation Formula for a 40-Year Old										
Policy			Tactical Models			Actual Weight				
SPY	TLT	GLD	SPY	TLT	GLD	SPY	TLT	GLD	BND	MMkt
60%	20%	20%	-50%	100%	100%	-30%	20%	20%	60%	30%
60%	20%	20%	-50%	0%	100%	-30%	0%	20%	0%	110%
60%	20%	20%	-50%	100%	0%	-30%	20%	0%	60%	50%
60%	20%	20%	-50%	0%	0%	-30%	0%	0%	0%	130%
60%	20%	20%	0%	100%	100%	0%	20%	20%	60%	0%
60%	20%	20%	0%	0%	100%	0%	0%	20%	0%	80%
60%	20%	20%	0%	100%	0%	0%	20%	0%	60%	20%
60%	20%	20%	0%	0%	0%	0%	0%	0%	0%	100%
60%	20%	20%	50%	100%	100%	30%	20%	20%	30%	0%
60%	20%	20%	50%	0%	100%	30%	0%	20%	0%	50%
60%	20%	20%	50%	100%	0%	30%	20%	0%	50%	0%
60%	20%	20%	50%	0%	0%	30%	0%	0%	0%	70%
60%	20%	20%	100%	100%	100%	60%	20%	20%	0%	0%
60%	20%	20%	100%	0%	100%	60%	0%	20%	0%	20%
60%	20%	20%	100%	100%	0%	60%	20%	0%	20%	0%
60%	20%	20%	100%	0%	0%	60%	0%	0%	0%	40%
60%	20%	20%	150%	100%	100%	90%	20%	20%	0%	-30%
60%	20%	20%	150%	0%	100%	90%	0%	20%	0%	-10%
60%	20%	20%	150%	100%	0%	90%	20%	0%	0%	-10%
60%	20%	20%	150%	0%	0%	90%	0%	0%	0%	10%
60%	20%	20%	200%	100%	100%	120%	20%	20%	0%	-60%
60%	20%	20%	200%	0%	100%	120%	0%	20%	0%	-40%
60%	20%	20%	200%	100%	0%	120%	20%	0%	0%	-40%
60%	20%	20%	200%	0%	0%	120%	0%	0%	0%	-20%

Table 6

Asset Allocation Formula for a 50-Year Old										
Policy			Tactical Models			Actual Weight				
SPY	TLT	GLD	SPY	TLT	GLD	SPY	TLT	GLD	BND	MMkt
40%	20%	20%	-50%	100%	100%	-20%	20%	20%	40%	40%
40%	20%	20%	-50%	0%	100%	-20%	0%	20%	0%	100%
40%	20%	20%	-50%	100%	0%	-20%	20%	0%	40%	60%
40%	20%	20%	-50%	0%	0%	-20%	0%	0%	0%	120%
40%	20%	20%	0%	100%	100%	0%	20%	20%	40%	20%
40%	20%	20%	0%	0%	100%	0%	0%	20%	0%	80%
40%	20%	20%	0%	100%	0%	0%	20%	0%	40%	40%
40%	20%	20%	0%	0%	0%	0%	0%	0%	0%	100%
40%	20%	20%	50%	100%	100%	20%	20%	20%	30%	10%
40%	20%	20%	50%	0%	100%	20%	0%	20%	0%	60%
40%	20%	20%	50%	100%	0%	20%	20%	0%	40%	20%
40%	20%	20%	50%	0%	0%	20%	0%	0%	0%	80%
40%	20%	20%	100%	100%	100%	40%	20%	20%	0%	20%
40%	20%	20%	100%	0%	100%	40%	0%	20%	0%	40%
40%	20%	20%	100%	100%	0%	40%	20%	0%	20%	20%
40%	20%	20%	100%	0%	0%	40%	0%	0%	0%	60%
40%	20%	20%	150%	100%	100%	60%	20%	20%	0%	0%
40%	20%	20%	150%	0%	100%	60%	0%	20%	0%	20%
40%	20%	20%	150%	100%	0%	60%	20%	0%	5%	15%
40%	20%	20%	150%	0%	0%	60%	0%	0%	0%	40%
40%	20%	20%	200%	100%	100%	80%	20%	20%	0%	-20%
40%	20%	20%	200%	0%	100%	80%	0%	20%	0%	0%
40%	20%	20%	200%	100%	0%	80%	20%	0%	0%	0%
40%	20%	20%	200%	0%	0%	80%	0%	0%	0%	20%

Table 7

Asset Allocation Formula for a 60-Year Old										
Policy			Tactical Models			Actual Weight				
SPY	TLT	GLD	SPY	TLT	GLD	SPY	TLT	GLD	BND	MMkt
30%	30%	10%	-50%	100%	100%	-15%	30%	10%	30%	45%
30%	30%	10%	-50%	0%	100%	-15%	0%	10%	0%	105%
30%	30%	10%	-50%	100%	0%	-15%	30%	0%	30%	55%
30%	30%	10%	-50%	0%	0%	-15%	0%	0%	0%	115%
30%	30%	10%	0%	100%	100%	0%	30%	10%	30%	30%
30%	30%	10%	0%	0%	100%	0%	0%	10%	0%	90%
30%	30%	10%	0%	100%	0%	0%	30%	0%	30%	40%
30%	30%	10%	0%	0%	0%	0%	0%	0%	0%	100%
30%	30%	10%	50%	100%	100%	15%	30%	10%	30%	15%
30%	30%	10%	50%	0%	100%	15%	0%	10%	0%	75%
30%	30%	10%	50%	100%	0%	15%	30%	0%	30%	25%
30%	30%	10%	50%	0%	0%	15%	0%	0%	0%	85%
30%	30%	10%	100%	100%	100%	30%	30%	10%	10%	20%
30%	30%	10%	100%	0%	100%	30%	0%	10%	0%	60%
30%	30%	10%	100%	100%	0%	30%	30%	0%	30%	10%
30%	30%	10%	100%	0%	0%	30%	0%	0%	0%	70%
30%	30%	10%	150%	100%	100%	45%	30%	10%	15%	0%
30%	30%	10%	150%	0%	100%	45%	0%	10%	0%	45%
30%	30%	10%	150%	100%	0%	45%	30%	0%	5%	20%
30%	30%	10%	150%	0%	0%	45%	0%	0%	0%	55%
30%	30%	10%	200%	100%	100%	60%	30%	10%	0%	0%
30%	30%	10%	200%	0%	100%	60%	0%	10%	0%	30%
30%	30%	10%	200%	100%	0%	60%	30%	0%	20%	-10%
30%	30%	10%	200%	0%	0%	60%	0%	0%	0%	40%

Table 8

Asset Allocation Formula for a 70-Year Old										
Policy			Tactical Models			Actual Weight				
SPY	TLT	GLD	SPY	TLT	GLD	SPY	TLT	GLD	BND	MMkt
20%	30%	10%	-50%	100%	100%	-10%	30%	10%	20%	50%
20%	30%	10%	-50%	0%	100%	-10%	0%	10%	0%	100%
20%	30%	10%	-50%	100%	0%	-10%	30%	0%	20%	60%
20%	30%	10%	-50%	0%	0%	-10%	0%	0%	0%	110%
20%	30%	10%	0%	100%	100%	0%	30%	10%	20%	40%
20%	30%	10%	0%	0%	100%	0%	0%	10%	0%	90%
20%	30%	10%	0%	100%	0%	0%	30%	0%	20%	50%
20%	30%	10%	0%	0%	0%	0%	0%	0%	0%	100%
20%	30%	10%	50%	100%	100%	10%	30%	10%	10%	40%
20%	30%	10%	50%	0%	100%	10%	0%	10%	0%	80%
20%	30%	10%	50%	100%	0%	10%	30%	0%	20%	40%
20%	30%	10%	50%	0%	0%	10%	0%	0%	0%	90%
20%	30%	10%	100%	100%	100%	20%	30%	10%	0%	40%
20%	30%	10%	100%	0%	100%	20%	0%	10%	0%	70%
20%	30%	10%	100%	100%	0%	20%	30%	0%	10%	40%
20%	30%	10%	100%	0%	0%	20%	0%	0%	0%	80%
20%	30%	10%	150%	100%	100%	30%	30%	10%	0%	30%
20%	30%	10%	150%	0%	100%	30%	0%	10%	0%	60%
20%	30%	10%	150%	100%	0%	30%	30%	0%	0%	40%
20%	30%	10%	150%	0%	0%	30%	0%	0%	0%	70%
20%	30%	10%	200%	100%	100%	40%	30%	10%	0%	20%
20%	30%	10%	200%	0%	100%	40%	0%	10%	0%	50%
20%	30%	10%	200%	100%	0%	40%	30%	0%	0%	30%
20%	30%	10%	200%	0%	0%	40%	0%	0%	0%	60%

Table 9

| Asset Allocation Formula for a 80-Year Old | | | | | | | | | | |
| Policy | | | Tactical Models | | | Actual Weight | | | | |
SPY	TLT	GLD	SPY	TLT	GLD	SPY	TLT	GLD	BND	MMkt
10%	30%	10%	-50%	100%	100%	-5%	10%	10%	10%	75%
10%	30%	10%	-50%	0%	100%	-5%	0%	10%	0%	95%
10%	30%	10%	-50%	100%	0%	-5%	30%	0%	10%	65%
10%	30%	10%	-50%	0%	0%	-5%	0%	0%	0%	105%
10%	30%	10%	0%	100%	100%	0%	30%	10%	10%	50%
10%	30%	10%	0%	0%	100%	0%	0%	10%	0%	90%
10%	30%	10%	0%	100%	0%	0%	30%	0%	10%	60%
10%	30%	10%	0%	0%	0%	0%	0%	0%	0%	100%
10%	30%	10%	50%	100%	100%	5%	30%	10%	5%	50%
10%	30%	10%	50%	0%	100%	5%	0%	10%	0%	85%
10%	30%	10%	50%	100%	0%	5%	30%	0%	15%	50%
10%	30%	10%	50%	0%	0%	5%	0%	0%	0%	95%
10%	30%	10%	100%	100%	100%	10%	30%	10%	0%	50%
10%	30%	10%	100%	0%	100%	10%	0%	10%	0%	80%
10%	30%	10%	100%	100%	0%	10%	30%	0%	10%	50%
10%	30%	10%	100%	0%	0%	10%	0%	0%	0%	90%
10%	30%	10%	150%	100%	100%	15%	30%	10%	0%	45%
10%	30%	10%	150%	0%	100%	15%	0%	10%	0%	75%
10%	30%	10%	150%	100%	0%	15%	30%	0%	5%	50%
10%	30%	10%	150%	0%	0%	15%	0%	0%	0%	85%
10%	30%	10%	200%	100%	100%	20%	30%	10%	0%	40%
10%	30%	10%	200%	0%	100%	20%	0%	10%	0%	70%
10%	30%	10%	200%	100%	0%	20%	30%	0%	0%	50%
10%	30%	10%	200%	0%	0%	20%	0%	0%	0%	80%

Table 10

REFERENCES

Barber, Brad M. and Heath, Chip and Odean, Terrance, *Good Reasons Sell: Reason-Based Choice Among Group and Individual Investors in the Stock Market*. Management Science, vol. 49, no. 12, pp. 1636-1652, December 2003.

Befumo, Randy, and Alex Schay. "History of the Dow," Fool.com (http://www.fool.com/DDow/HistoryOfTheDow5.htm).

Blackrock. December 2012. "Chart of the Week," BlackRock website (https://www2.blackrock.com/us/financial-professionals/market-insight/chart-of-the-week/volatility-propels-emotional-investing).

Choi, James. September 2000. *The Value-Line Enigma: Sum of Known Parts?*, Journal of Financial and Quantitative Analysis, vol. 35, no. 3. Seattle, WA: School of Business, University of Washington.

Fischer, David Hackett. 1996. *The Great Wave: Price Revolutions and the Rhythm of History*. New York: Oxford University Press.

Friedman, Milton, and Ana Schwartz. 1963. *A Monetary History of the United States 1867–1960*. Princeton, NJ: Princeton University Press.

Gray, Wes. May 2011. "How 'Magic' is the Magic Formula?," Empirical Finance Blog (http://blog.empiricalfinancellc.com/2011/05/how-magic-is-the-magic-formula/).

Greenblatt, Joel. 2005. *The Little Book That Beats the Market*. Hoboken, NJ: Wiley & Sons.

Harvey, Louis. 2013. *Quantitative Analysis of Investor Behavior*. Boston, MA: Dalbar.

Lynch, Peter. 1989. *One Up on Wall Street.* New York: Simon & Schuster.

Reeves, Jeff. May 2012. *Why Warren Buffett Hates Gold.* Investorplace. com (http://investorplace.com/2012/05/why-warren-buffett-hates-gold/#.UokxqlAo6ig).

ABOUT THE AUTHOR

Michael Allen was a number-one-rated analyst for a leading international investment bank where he won acclaim from clients for his ability to see trouble brewing well before others and to see positive turnarounds when others were still negative. He later took on leadership roles at two multibillion-dollar hedge funds where he successfully bridged the gap between fundamental and quantitative analysis and further developed his unique multidiscipline style of investment. Upon returning to the US, he founded Aston Research, which provides advice to businesses and individuals on Asian-based investments and on asset allocation strategies.